Advanc

MW00984510

"Bob Reby addresses the age-old question, 'Do you work to live or live to work?' He understands that financial decisions are made with the big picture in mind."

—**STEVE SOKOL**, Esq., founder and president of Sokol Associates

"If you are interested in having your money work for you, financial freedom, financial independence, and financial peace of mind, *Wealth Redefined* is a must read."

—**JONATHAN R. ELYACHAR,**
chairman of the board, Elyachar Properties

"As a father of four, and with aging parents, this is a must read. Absolutely masterful."

—**TODD WYMBS**, owner of Wymbs, Inc.

"*Wealth Redefined* addresses family, relationships, and rewarding life choices in the same tone as income, prosperity, and wealth and sets the standard as to how all books of this nature should be penned. Setting a goal of how to achieve *your* vision of wealth and setting a course of action to realize that goal is priceless, and so is the advice in this book."

—**JEFFREY JOWDY**, Esq., Jowdy & Jowdy,
a Connecticut and New York law firm

"I loved reading *Wealth Redefined*. Bob Reby offers new insight and advice on having a healthy relationship with money. It's a must read for everyone at any age."

—**RICH FOUDY**, happily retired executive

Wealth
Redefined

Wealth Redefined

CHARTING THE WAY TO PERSONAL AND FINANCIAL FREEDOM

BOB REBY

WITH GREGG RUAIS

RIVER GROVE
BOOKS

Published by River Grove Books
Austin, TX
www.rivergrovebooks.com

Distributed by River Grove Books

Design and composition by Greenleaf Book Group and Kim Lance
Cover design by Greenleaf Book Group and Kim Lance
Image Copyright Andrekart Photography, 2017. Used under license from Shutterstock.com;
Polka Dot Images/Thinkstock,

Cataloging-in-Publication data is available.

Print ISBN: 978-1-63299-125-6

eBook ISBN: 978-1-63299-126-3

First Edition

*This book is dedicated to all the people that
have touched my life and have taught me that
"the best way to predict the future, is to create it yourself."*

*And to my wife, Mary,
thank you for your patience and loving support.*

Contents

Wealth Redefined

"It's good to have money and the things that money can buy,
but it's good, too, to check up once in a while and make sure
that you haven't lost the things that money can't buy."

—GEORGE HORACE LORIMER

FOR MOST PEOPLE, the word *wealth* conjures images of material possessions and luxury: fancy jewelry, exotic automobiles, opulent living quarters, and vacations in Southern France. To become wealthy is the pinnacle of the iconic American Dream. When you can afford the best of everything you want—that big house with the perfect white picket fence, that boat docked in the harbor—you get to live happily ever after, carefree.

That may be the traditional vision of wealth, but it hasn't been my experience.

One thing I've learned over the past several decades as a Certified Financial Planner is that wealth means different things to different people. Most of the time, when we speak about wealth we're talking about money. However, over the years, I've seen some of our clients who live very modestly feel extremely wealthy because they spend all kinds of free time with their lovely grandchildren or pursuing their personal passions. I've also seen very financially wealthy people with many millions of dollars who feel isolated and lonely in their own world of money.

Wealth is more than money. It encompasses many other things in life that are not counted in dollars and cents. Your health, relationships, and family are all components of wealth. These things generally do not cost anything, but they play a pivotal role in your life. If you're healthy and have an abundance of genuine relationships with family and friends, you would probably never trade those things for material wealth. That's the kind of wealth most people really need and desire, even if they believe material wealth is their ultimate goal.

Living well is more about improving the quality of your life rather than spending money on a lot of stuff. A good example of this is a hardworking executive who works eighty hours a week to earn $200,000 per year so that he can maintain his mortgage and lifestyle, but may have less freedom than the self-employed business owner who works twenty hours a week, earns $50,000, has zero debts, minimal expenses, and more time to focus on his passions, family, friends, and interests.

Quality of life is different for everyone. For some people, this means spending more time with their grandkids on their laps. For others, quality of life means traveling the world and experiencing new cultures. Many people consider an early retirement to be the ultimate goal. Others are too passionate about their careers to even think about retirement.

Wealth Redefined is the culmination of over thirty years of experience advising people on the wealth management philosophies and belief systems that have helped many families achieve financial peace of mind. Money touches nearly every aspect of our lives, but it's critical to view it as a means to an end, not the end in and of itself.

In my opinion, members of the financial media get it wrong when they view material wealth as the end goal and then use their platform to give out advice intended for everybody. For example, they may give advice like "This is why I hate annuities and you should, too" or "Do not eat out at a restaurant for one month." The people who've made these statements may have had valid points about the financial *downside* of annuities or eating at restaurants, but in my experience this is not advice that can be given without a clearer understanding of a person's particular situation, personality, and goals. It certainly does not apply to everyone in America.

For the most part, I agree that annuities are high-priced and commonly misused. However, the higher cost may be a small price to pay for some people who cannot stomach market volatility. Furthermore, eating out at restaurants may be your favorite thing in the world. In that case, giving it up entirely is no way to live; if you need to cut back on spending to remain within your "spending speed limit," do so in other areas where it has less of an impact on your enjoyment of life.

Of course, as a financial advisor, I spend a lot of my time helping clients figure out how to maximize material wealth. But I would be doing them a great disservice if I treated money as the endgame. Money is for security and peace of mind. Beyond that, there's no established universal formula on what you should do with your money. Is having as much money as possible really a worthy goal? Money is merely green pieces of paper and digits on an account statement. It's not necessarily how much you have but what you do with it that counts. Once you have enough to take care of your own basic needs for security and peace of mind, it's time to spend or invest that money in being truly wealthy.

Wealth Is about Being Happy

Wealth redefined is more than a tagline that reflects my personal beliefs. It's also backed by evidence and research. A seventy-five-year study by Harvard psychiatrist George Vaillant[1] proves that more money does not always make us happier. In fact, the correlation between higher income and more happiness plateaus at around $75,000 per year.

This does not mean that $75,000 a year is the magic number for everyone. We're all different personality-wise, and practical factors such as cost of living in your geographic area will affect your own magic number. But that number is probably lower than you would have assumed. More important than income, the study found, is having meaningful relationships with family and friends and a meaningful connection to your work.

The traditional model of wealth building is to go after promotions, grow income, and save and invest to grow your money. Wealth redefined means that we should strive to achieve the right balance in our lives that *also* takes into consideration whether we're spending our time and our money on the right things.

---

1   George Bradt, "The Secret of Happiness Revealed by Harvard Study," *Forbes*, May 27, 2015, http://www.forbes.com/sites/georgebradt/2015/05/27/the-secret-of-happiness-revealed-by-harvard -study/#7284f0f32c9f.

For most people, finding the right balance requires introspection and self-knowledge in addition to creative financial planning. Are you spending enough quality time with your family and friends? Is your job aligned with your personal values and passions? Do you have the time and resources to pursue any hobbies you find personally rewarding? Finally, are your decisions with money helping you move in the right directions in these areas?

Don't focus on money first and assume everything will fall into place after that. Focus instead on what true wealth means to *you* and then build your financial strategies around that. For example, let's say that your idea of wealth is to experience many distant cultures and meet many kinds of different people during your life. First, quantify some objectives that support this goal. This could be visiting one new state and one new country for one week each year. Now, estimate how much this would cost you on a timeline, factoring inflation for future years. If you've identified this as your top goal, the pinnacle of what wealth means to you, build the rest of your financial decisions to support this: the career you pursue, the day-to-day living expenses you take on, and how much money you put away in savings.

The key to achieving the wealth of experiences you're after will be to either earn enough income so that you can travel at your leisure or to avoid taking on a lifestyle that would make travel cost-prohibitive. You should also factor in that at some point you may want to stop working, at least full time, and you'll want enough money in investments to eventually transition from working for your money to having your money work for you. This planning takes time and effort, but you can see how, in this example, you are making your money work for you in a meaningful way instead of reaching for traditional goals and then trying to squeeze in the time and money for your passions.

As you map out your financial future, don't start with how much money you can afford to save. Start at the end. Have a goal line that you'll strive to reach. Take some time to think about it. Write out your ideal lifestyle, prioritize according to what you really need to be happy, and distinguish between those necessities and the "nice-to-haves." You may think of your children and grandchildren and decide leaving a legacy is foremost to you. How you spend your time will probably be a priority as well. This is how you start to define the purpose of your assets, the purpose of your money, and even how to invest your time.

Wealth Is about Freedom

All the money in the world means nothing if you don't have the ability to spend it as you wish, or if it's tied up in debts and liabilities. Freedom is the ability to make decisions on your own and determine what you do and when you do it.

It's better to work because you want to than to work because you have to. I'm always impressed by people in their seventies and eighties who are financially independent by every definition that you can think of, but they still love their work. It keeps them very active mentally and emotionally and even helps them physically. Other people transition from a career where they make a lot of money to working full time making less money, following their passion or even working for free for a charity or nonprofit.

This type of freedom—for most people—will require a certain amount of traditional wealth accumulation. Ultimately, however, I believe financial independence is truly about making the transition from working for your money to having *your money work for you*. Once you've accumulated enough money through traditional wealth-building to be able to leverage your assets to create predictable streams of income that will support your lifestyle, you can make decisions on your own terms, not someone else's. You're in the driver's seat on the road to true wealth.

Wealth Is about Peace of Mind

Money is an emotional topic. On the one hand, we can agree that money isn't everything. On the other, your life savings represents decades of hard work. It's what your family relies on for stability and comfort. It may even be your children's or grandchildren's college education or legacy. For these reasons and many others, financial worry can keep you up at night no matter how high your income or how large your portfolio.

Being fearful of the next market downturn, losing your job or a big client, or running out of money after reaching retirement can sometimes be as restrictive and emotionally taxing as those things actually happening. When I work with clients to develop a financial plan or investment strategy, financial peace of mind is the ultimate goal. Unless you're comfortable and confident in the path forward, you probably will not stay the course of your plan, no matter how well constructed it is or how conclusive the evidence is that supports it.

As I'll cover later in this book, this emotional connection with your money can be incredibly destructive when you allow fear and greed to influence your decisions. Achieving financial peace of mind makes it much easier to remain calm and objective in your decisions and ultimately leads to greater financial and emotional health.

Because of the emotional component to money, achieving financial peace of mind may be the most complex problem in all of personal finance. The vast majority of people face financial tradeoffs in every investment, insurance, or planning decision they make. You're often balancing multiple goals and prioritizing. Whether it's buying a second home, downsizing, or simplifying your lifestyle to shed some costs you really don't need, I've found it's important to talk through these priorities and understand your options in order to be truly comfortable with your plan moving forward.

Once you've prioritized and decided which goals take precedence, you need an income strategy—not an investment strategy—to support these goals. Investments are part of your income strategy, but the exact performance of your portfolio is not as critical to your peace of mind as having predictable streams of income you can count on to support your lifestyle.

Balancing tradeoffs between your own peace of mind and helping family

As I mentioned, a big part of achieving financial peace of mind for many people is knowing that your children will be okay financially. However, with rising prices and taxes, particularly the high cost of a college education, it's harder than ever to support children without sacrificing your own quality of life.

Keep in mind that if you hand a child a million dollars, or even two million dollars, it won't necessarily last a lifetime—especially if they do not have the wealth skills to protect and grow their money with evidence-centered investment strategies.

I challenge clients in our meetings to really think about the tradeoffs between financial flexibility for themselves and being able to help their children. The process starts with simply asking questions.

Are you willing to work six more years to support your goal of paying for their college education or medical school? On the other hand, could these children who you've worked hard to educate and be a role model for share some of the education cost, so you could retire in six months instead of six years? Is that a trade-off you'd rather make?

A better gift than leaving an inheritance (and one that does not cost you anything) may be teaching your kids fundamental personal finance skills. Teach your kids, in concrete terms, how the 15% interest rate applied to their credit card balance can hurt their life-style if they don't have the discipline and the means to pay off their balances in full. Get them in the mindset of paying themselves first, thereby building discipline to live within their means. Today young adults are spending too much money relative to their income and savings (or lack thereof). It's a challenge to balance living the lifestyle that they aspire to versus making necessary sacrifices.

If your children are of working age, I recommend telling them this: If you're not investing, if you're not having your money put to work as hard as you're working for it, it's a mistake that can hurt your future. And as important as it is to invest your money, it's even more important to invest in yourself and be marketable in today's fast-moving, fast-paced world.

I realize that not all millennials are ready to make lifestyle sacri-fices. In the era we live in, it's understandable why they may not have trust in financial institutions and financial markets; this lack of trust may make them reluctant to believe that sacrificing now by investing their money will pay off in the long run. However, consider putting it in these terms:

- If you save $5 per day by not eating out for lunch and instead invest that money to earn a conservative 6% return, you end up with more than $17,000 in ten years and more than $100,000 in thirty years.

- By brewing your own coffee instead of spending $2 per day and investing the savings, you accumulate more than $10,000 over ten years and more than $60,000 over thirty years.

- If you save and invest $7.30 per day (the average cost of a pack of cigarettes), your ten-year savings would be more than $37,000 over ten years and more than $220,000 over thirty years.

This math works for any small change in your daily spending. That's the magic of compounding interest, and the younger you are, the more this works in your favor. And for those who are skeptical of financial markets, even factoring in the impact of the Great Recession, markets have *always* gone up over the long run.

To be intellectually honest, I admit that the figures above look greater than they actually are, because inflation will reduce the future value of those sums of money. But these aren't small numbers, and even factoring in inflation, your child may be more willing to make some minor lifestyle adjustments now when they consider the purchasing power of their money after the magic of compounding interest has been applied.

When helping your children choose their college courses or major, take a step back and consider the spendable income their degree can offer over a lifetime. Calculating the high cost and years of education, studies show that a doctor may have only $500 a year more in spending money than a plumber.[2]

It's not advisable to choose a career solely because of money, because the graduates who do well in life are those armed with talent and ambition, not necessarily those who chose the major that pays the most. Furthermore, some people simply are not a good fit for

2   William Baldwin, "The 10 Steps to Make Your Kid a Millionaire," *Forbes*, June, 8, 2011, http://www.forbes .com/forbes/2011/0627/money-guide-11-kotlikoff-roth-ira-mutual-fund-kid-millionaire.html

certain careers. (I personally learned in college that I was not born to be an engineer, but I was very strong at finance.) The point is to help your children carefully consider various education options to make sure they won't end up with a huge debt by graduation time relative to the income they can expect.

Building wealth starts with having the right mindset—a viewpoint that seeks a clear view of the future, an honest understanding of the current situation, and a strategic approach on how to get from where you are now to where you want to be. Instilling this mindset can be the greatest gift of all to a child who you'd like to be financially independent some day.

Peace of mind challenge: Avoid being a burden to loved ones

I have talked to thousands of families during my career, and something that comes up a lot is that people do not want to become a burden to their loved ones. This doesn't mean the same thing for everybody, but I do believe the whole concept of maintaining your dignity as you age is critical for many people. They want peace of mind in knowing they won't have to rely on their children or their grandchildren for more help than they are comfortable asking for.

Issues we often do not like to think about, like independent living, assisted living facilities, and long-term care, are important for planning purposes when determining how much money you need to achieve financial independence. Like many other advisors, I used to talk about "longevity risk" a lot, which is living longer than you're supposed to (statistically).

With today's improvements to health care, I almost always assume, as if it were a fact, that at least one person in a married couple will live into their nineties or older. Without making this assumption, my clients would run the risk of running out of money, nearly everyone's greatest financial fear.

The ability to address the issue of maintaining independence as you age essentially comes down to the three factors that influence just about everything: time, resources, and willingness to make tradeoffs. The more time you have to plan, the more flexibility you'll have to insure yourself against independence risk or to build the assets to self-insure. The more money you have, the more options you'll have available to you. And finally, what are you willing to give up as a tradeoff?

How to Achieve *Your* Vision of Wealth

At this point, I hope I've convinced you that there's no set-in-stone dollar amount to which we all must aspire to be considered wealthy. The age-old question of "How much money do I need to retire?" should be replaced with "What does financial independence mean to me, and how do I achieve it?"

This book will cover this question, with a particular focus on conservative financial planning strategies and evidence-centered investing that will help you transition from working for your money to having your money work for you. I'll discuss the roadblocks you'll probably encounter on your road to financial independence, how Wall Street is failing Main Street, and relevant case studies illustrating how people become *their* idea of wealthy.

1

Wall Street vs. Main Street

WHAT THE BIG BANKS AND BROKERAGE FIRMS DON'T WANT YOU TO KNOW

> "Lesson number one: Don't underestimate
> the other guy's greed."
> —**FRANK LOPEZ, *SCARFACE* (1983)**

WHEN YOU NEED professional financial advice, how do you know who you can trust? A traditional approach is to turn to Wall Street institutions: dominant banks with wealth management divisions that have given advice to many generations of Americans. On the surface, this seems like a safe bet. These banks spend millions conducting research on financial markets and developing complex algorithms to guide their buy-sell decisions. They hire and groom the smartest Ivy League graduates as analysts, and the advisors present you with a polished proposal, complete with beautiful charts and graphs that make it look like they have money down to a science.

Too frequently in my career, however, I've seen people from Main Street get bad or incomplete financial advice from these Wall Street institutions. The advice often lacks transparency, results in the client paying commission fees that are too high, and overlooks the tax consequences of where and how they invest their money. Depending on the individual, the added expenses and unnecessary taxes they pay may amount to tens of thousands per year. Accumulated over a lifetime, it's not an exaggeration to say these unnecessary costs may shave five years off your retirement. It may also be the difference between running out of money and sustaining a good lifestyle.

Perhaps even more costly than the unnecessary fees and taxes Main Street ends up paying as a result of their advice from Wall Street is *the advice they aren't getting*. Most people I sit down with who have an advisor at a major bank are not getting advice on critical topics such as the type of insurance they should buy, exactly how much money they can afford to spend each year without running out of money, and how and when to claim Social Security and Medicare. These areas of personal finance are arguably as important if not more important than the funds you invest in. Ignoring these issues may not result in losing a few percentage points of earnings from your portfolio, but it may result in a complete loss of financial independence.

To protect yourself and your family against this poor or incomplete advice, it's critical to know where Wall Street leads Main Street astray, the reasons for the poor or incomplete advice being given, and how you can identify the warning signs that are revealed when an advisor isn't giving you the quality of advice you deserve.

Is Your Advisor Putting Your Interests Ahead of His Own?

Many people are surprised that half of professional money managers do not invest their own money in the same portfolios they build for others. This is a startling figure that begs the question, *Why not?* If they believe in these portfolios and investments enough to sell them to the public, why wouldn't they invest their own money in them?

Unfortunately, Wall Street often has a conflict of interest with its clients. Contrary to popular opinion, many advisors at these large banks are not required to put their clients' interests ahead of their own when giving financial advice. Some advisors may recommend investments that include fees because those are the investments that pay them commissions. It's hard to blame them for doing what they need to do in order to pay the bills and feed their families, but it's also difficult to trust the advice when they get paid more for selling you an investment that's *worse* for your family.

The term *advisor* has become a misleading job title in many cases. Registered representatives at these banks used to be called *stockbrokers*, a term that's been stigmatized through pop culture and mainstream media. Now just about everyone who sells securities has the benign title of *financial advisor*, or simply *vice president*, even though the job description hasn't changed much.

Many of these brokers are not fiduciaries to their clients. This means they are held to a lesser standard called *suitability*, which means the investment strategy they recommend to clients must meet the objectives of the investor. Suitability, however, does not mean that the investments recommended are the ones *most likely* to help an investor reach their objectives or even that the advisor selling the securities believes that it is the best investment for the client.

This suitability standard allows the advisor to sell securities and funds with unnecessarily high fees, even though there is no correlation between fund expenses and fund performance. In some instances, the same exact investments may be available for no fee, but the client never sees those opportunities because the advisor cannot earn a commission from them.

There are also hybrid situations where the advisor *almost* puts your interests first, but not completely. Large investment banks underwrite certain financial products, such as tax-free municipal bonds or master limited partnerships. They earn more profit from selling products they underwrite themselves, because they make money through multiple channels that way. So there might have been a better tax-free municipal bond for you to own, but you never got a chance to actually see it because your advisor may have an adverse incentive to sell you the one being distributed by the company itself. The advisor may not be selling you something that's bad for you—as a tax-free municipal bond may be what you need—but the particular one sold to you was not the best of its class.

The first step to safeguarding against this type of conflict of interest is to understand the type of financial advisor you're working with and the extent of his or her legal obligations to you. To avoid the conflict of interest inherent in working with a commission-based broker, you can work with a financial advisor who has a fiduciary duty to put your interests first, a Registered Investment Advisor (RIA) or a Certified Financial Planner (CFP). Being independent, RIAs have a wide universe of products to make available to you, and they are obligated to recommend the best option for you. A Certified Financial Planner is held to an even higher standard, including professional experience requirements, ethics coursework, and continuing education.

Now, it's important to remember that while fiduciaries are held to a higher standard, this does not mean that they necessarily have more integrity or ethics. There are fiduciaries who do not act in a fiduciary way. Bernie Madoff was a fiduciary.

What's more important than a title, of course, is that that the advisor is *acting* in a fiduciary way and giving advice in the spirit of "What I would do if I were you." This should be the golden rule of the financial advisory industry.

How do you know if an advisor meets this standard? Here are a few questions you can ask yourself about your current advisor (or questions to ask a prospective advisor) in order to determine whether the advice you're getting is in your best interests and truly comprehensive:

- Does your advisor talk to you about the tax ramifications of where you put your money and when and how you take it out?

- Does your advisor give advice based on your personal values, dreams, and goals for both you and your family?

- Does your advisor offer advice beyond assets under management, such as your overall spending rate, the risks to your lifestyle, and Social Security and Medicare selections?

- Does your advisor proactively communicate with you during recessions or market downturns and coach you away from emotional investing based on fear and greed?

If you answered yes to these questions, you're likely working with an advisor who's looking after your best interests. If not, you probably have holes in your current financial plan and would benefit from more comprehensive advice.

The following sections of this chapter are dedicated to each question, why it's important, and how your answer helps reveal the quality of the advice you're getting.

Does Your Advisor Talk about the Tax Ramifications of What You Do with Your Money?

Taxes are one of the most significant expenses in nearly any household. For most retired households, it's the greatest expense. Yet most advisors do not review their clients' tax returns each year to help save money on taxes, increase cash flow, and improve quality of life.

If advice on how to maximize post-tax income does not come from a financial advisor, who will it come from? Most accountants are hired to review your income *after* your investment strategy has been in place. Their focus, generally, is minimizing your tax bill after the fact. The best accountants may advise you on how to minimize taxes on your investment income going forward, but they aren't the ones executing trades for you. That responsibility falls on your advisor (or you, if you handle your own investing).

Here are a few ways an advisor who's giving comprehensive fiduciary advice can help reduce your income taxes:

Advise how to invest your assets to minimize your current income taxes

There is almost always room for improvement when it comes to minimizing your income taxes, especially if you're earning more than you're spending. Once you have enough cash reserves for emergencies and unexpected expenses, it's usually to your advantage to invest your surplus in a qualified retirement account, which means you get to invest your pretax income and defer taxes until it's time to withdraw funds in retirement. To minimize income taxes preretirement while you're in the wealth accumulation phase, maximize 401(k) or Traditional IRA contributions. This is really simple advice that has an immediate positive impact, but many advisors will overlook the opportunity.

Advise how to invest your assets to minimize income taxes in retirement

As you approach retirement, it's often a good idea to also have an account outside of your retirement accounts. How can this be used to your advantage? Having a standard non-retirement account may reduce your income taxes when you're withdrawing from your assets in retirement. Gains from these non-retirement accounts may be taxed as long-term capital gains, which is lower than the tax rate on ordinary income. In addition, your non-retirement account may have a loss, which enables *loss harvesting* at the end of the year. Loss harvesting means you sell assets at a loss, and use that loss to offset your other income. This minimizes your income tax bill in a way that having a 401(k) alone cannot.

While I realize this advice may seem to contradict my first point about the advantages of retirement accounts, this is a delicate balancing act that should not be implemented without thought and strategy.

Telling you when and how much to withdraw from an IRA account

There is really nothing worse than finding out after you've made a decision that you've thrown away thousands of dollars unnecessarily.

After you've reached the minimum distribution age of 59 ½ to withdraw from qualified retirement accounts, it's critical to consider the income tax ramifications of your withdrawals. Because you contribute to these retirement accounts with pretax money and your contributions grow tax-free, your distributions are taxed as ordinary income. Income taxes are progressive, and all of your ordinary income counts; so if you withdraw too much too soon, you'll end up in a higher tax bracket. This affects all of your income streams. On the other hand, if you take less than your required minimum distribution, you may pay a penalty later for not taking it sooner. A true Certified Financial Planner will help you avoid making these mistakes.

Choosing how to take an inherited legacy

When your children inherit a legacy, how they take it can result in significant tax savings. An advisor should give sound advice on the tax ramifications of taking the inheritance in a lump sum, deferred over five years, or spread out over a lifetime. Keep in mind that estate planning is a highly specialized field. Financial advisors should know about the topic, but almost none of us—myself included—know everything there is to know. Good advisors recognize their own limitations and will have a network of specialists to whom they can refer you for more advanced advice.

Does Your Advisor Give Good Advice?

Having a comprehensive financial plan is not a goal in and of itself. What matters most is everything that comes with it: reduced anxiety over money, more confidence in knowing the future, and the freedom to pursue your passions. A financial advisor who doesn't first take the time to learn about you, your family, and what you value and love the most cannot devise a plan that's right for you . . . unless he or she happens to guess correctly about these things.

To illustrate how a sound financial plan changes with individual needs and preferences, here are three hypothetical situations, all of which include investible assets of $750,000 at the time of retirement. Note that the dollar amount here is not as important as the process of identifying goals, prioritizing based on your values, and developing a financial plan that best utilizes the resources available to you to achieve your goals. This process is relevant whether you have a hundred thousand, one million, or ten million.

Family #1

- *Investible Assets*: $750,000

- *Family Situation:* Three successful children with high income for whom an inheritance would be "nice to have" but not at all necessary.

- *Lifestyle Goals:* Living near family in the tristate area during spring, summer, and fall, but likes to stay in Florida during the winters. Enjoys traveling and loves visiting Europe.

- *Financial Strategy:* Withdraw 6% of total investible assets ($45,000) each year to cover living expenses (along with Social Security income), and keep the remaining 95% in a 60%–40% mix between equity investments and fixed-income investments to maintain long-term growth.

The 6% "speed limit" on withdrawals exceeds the 4% rule of thumb because the couple recognizes that as they age, their ability to travel may become limited and they are willing to make the tradeoff of having lower income capability in the future in order to see as much of the world as possible while they are still young enough to do it. In addition, they are confident their children do not need an inheritance in order to achieve their own financial independence. Due to inflation, every five years they will adjust the withdrawal allowance up 15% to maintain the same quality of life (i.e., in five years, the withdrawal increases to $51,750).

Family #2

- *Investible Assets:* $750,000, and a business that can be sold for $150,000.

- *Family Situation:* Sixty-five-year-old couple with two children; the husband also has a thirty-year-old child with special needs from a previous marriage.

- *Lifestyle Goals:* It is important for the man to have peace of mind in knowing his special-needs child is cared for after he passes away. He also wants to ensure his two kids with his current wife are not excluded from the inheritance.

- *Financial Strategy:* Establish two separate trusts: one for the special-needs child and one for his two other children. The trust for the special-needs child should be held by a competent, trusted family member, who will distribute the money in a deferred manner to the special-needs child. This avoids inflating the net worth of the trustee, which could disqualify him from government benefits.

Family #3

- *Investible Assets:* $750,000

- *Family Situation:* Married couple with five children and $200,000 remaining on a mortgage at 5% interest. There is a family history of health issues on the father's side.

- *Lifestyle Goals:* Lead a comfortable lifestyle in their current home, spend time with family, and have peace of mind knowing that, should health issues arise, the rest of the family is protected.

- *Financial Strategy:* First, refinance the remaining mortgage into a fifteen-year loan with 3% interest. The cash the couple saves by not paying the mortgage off in full now can produce a higher rate of return than the 3% in interest they will pay. Plus, the 3% interest is a tax deduction. Second, the couple can purchase a long-term care insurance policy, which can cover the high cost of long-term care (on average, $350 per day in their home state of Connecticut) if the need arises and help keep the family finances stable.

Does Your Advisor Offer Advice beyond Assets Under Management?

To give the most helpful advice possible, a financial advisor should understand your entire financial picture, including assets not under management. Too many non-fiduciaries take the "out of sight, out of mind" approach to the financial assets they are not actively managing. This approach naturally results in the client getting incomplete advice.

Here are a few types of assets often held outside an advisory account that have a significant influence on a household's overall financial well-being:

- Personal property including real estate, fine collectibles, and vehicles

- Savings accounts held at a local bank

- Separate investing accounts

- Pensions that are paid monthly for life

- Future inheritances

- Your future expected Social Security benefit

An advisor who is truly looking out for your interests wants to know about these assets in order to give sound advice on topics such as the following:

- Should you pay your mortgage off now or use free cash to invest and claim mortgage interest as a deduction?

- Have you surpassed your "spending speed limit," and are you at risk of running out of money?

- Do you have the insurance coverage you need to protect against liabilities?

- Are you receiving Social Security and Medicare benefits?

Some of the most important financial advice you'll ever get will be unrelated to investing. Taking Social Security at the right time, for example, can add hundreds of thousands of dollars to your lifetime benefit, plus additional investment returns from receiving bigger or earlier checks (depending on which claiming strategy is right for you).

Another example of critical advice is how much you can safely spend each year without the risk of running out of money. I've seen many people slowly and painfully outlive their money, sometimes due to factors outside their control. However, in some cases it was simply due to a lack of advice on how their spending habits would affect their future income capability. While an advisor cannot withhold your money from you, it should be his or her fiduciary duty to advise you on the future ramifications of your current withdrawals and spending.

Does Your Advisor Proactively Communicate with You during Recessions or Market Downturns?

Did you know the average investor earns 5.2% less than the unmanaged S&P 500? This happens because the majority of investors allow fear and greed to factor into their decision-making. When the market goes up, many people get excited and buy; when the market tanks, they get scared and sell. This is a perfectly human reaction to the stock market. But it results in a situation where you end up buying high (after the boom has started) and selling low (prematurely, before the rebound). Over the long run, people who remain in a solid investment through rough economic patches keep the full historic returns of that investment. Part of a financial advisor's job is preparing clients for market volatility, both technically (through a diversified portfolio) and emotionally (by providing a calm and rational voice during economic volatility).

Advisors who simply take buy-sell orders because it's the easy way to keep clients happy are doing their clients a great disservice. Your advisor should provide ongoing coaching, reassuring you during recessions that you have a sound long-term strategy and are poised to capitalize during the upcoming rebound. During good times, your advisor should remind you that no bull market has ever lasted forever, prepare you emotionally for the next major downturn, and advise you on your spending, withdrawals, and asset allocation accordingly.

By helping clients avoid emotional investing, advisors can dramatically improve their clients' *return on behavior*. Markets have always gone up in the long run, but *investors' behavior* can be their own worst enemy—a concept I elaborate on in its own chapter.

I've detailed some of the most common oversights from Wall Street advisors and non-fiduciary advisors in general, but if you're getting incomplete advice (or no advice at all), how can you know whether you're doing well or not? The following chapter reveals exactly how to determine your overall financial health as it relates to your ability to achieve financial independence and sustain a good lifestyle

Keeping Score

SYSTEMATICALLY MINIMIZING
THE RISKS TO YOUR FAMILY'S LIFESTYLE

"Measurement is the first step that leads to control and
eventually to improvement. If you can't measure something,
you can't understand it. If you can't understand it, you can't
control it. If you can't control it, you can't improve it."
—H. JAMES HARRINGTON

DO YOU REMEMBER taking a practice test in high school or college that you knew you would not be graded on, or playing a sport without keeping score? Chances are, your sense of urgency was not as great as it would have been for the real test or for an athletic competition with a winner and a loser.

The same holds true in personal finance. When you keep score of how well you're doing, either on your own or with the help of a Certified Financial Planner, you end up saving more, investing better, and addressing those loose ends that leave you vulnerable to the risks that can derail your lifestyle.

You may already know a lot of what you need to know about money from reading books like this one. However, there's a big difference between knowing what you should be doing and actually doing it.

This chapter introduces a scorecard that will help you keep yourself accountable. I use this scorecard when developing financial plans for clients, and I've found that it's a great motivator. It shines light on financial vulnerabilities that you didn't see before and reminds you of financial homework that you knew you should be taking care of but were putting off because life kept getting in the way. People take it seriously when they have a score that represents a high likelihood of financial ruin.

It's called the *Lifestyle Sustainability Scorecard.* This risk assessment test measures how well you're minimizing the risks to your family's lifestyle on a scale of 0 to 100. There are fifteen risks in total, covering eight categories of personal finance.

The scorecard is designed to be flexible, adapting to your personal definition of wealth and what's most important to you.

Most people score between 40 and 60 on their initial assessment, which means your family's lifestyle is highly vulnerable to financial risks. After twelve to eighteen months, as long as your scorecard remains top of mind, you'll see your score rise dramatically. You can increase your score faster than that, depending on how you prioritize it in your life and which risks need addressing. (Some will take longer than others to shore up.)

Following is a sample scorecard illustrating a typical score of a family that has not yet engaged in the comprehensive financial planning process (60.45 out of 100). For the remainder of this chapter, I'll walk you through each section and explain how to score yourself. You may download my firm's scorecard template at no cost at www.rebyadvisors.com/scorecard to help follow along with this chapter, or take our online quiz to get a preliminary score calculated for you.

As shown, for each category, you'll rank yourself from one to ten. Since some categories are more important than others, you multiply that rank by the number in the multiplier column, and that's your score for that category. Then, add them all up for your total score.

CATEGORY	RANK (0 TO 10)	MULTIPLIER	SCORE
Life Policy Clarifier	0	0.3	0
Liquid Purpose Fund	10	0.2	2
Income Capability (contribution & withdrawal realities, Social Security & pension)	8	1.5	12
Income Protection (income protection strategy, health care strategy, personal liability protection, long-term care)	7.5	1.7	12.75
Income Tax Minimizer	8	1	8
Lifestyle Preservation Enhancer (return on behavior, investment policy statement, asset allocation, guaranteed income)	4.5	3	13.5

CATEGORY	RANK (0 TO 10)	MULTIPLIER	SCORE
Legacy Assurance (legacy assurance, documents, titling, beneficiaries)	4	1.8	7.2
Debt Management	10	0.5	5
Totals			60.45

Life Policy Clarifier:
Are Your Goals Documented and Clear?

A *Life Policy Clarifier* is a written document that outlines your financial lifestyle goals. Now, you're probably not surprised that a Certified Financial Planner would advocate that you should document your goals, so I'll keep this section concise and share two telling statistics:

- 48% of people with a financial plan describe themselves as living comfortably, while only 22% of non-planners say the same; and

- 50% of households earning $50,000–$99,999 per year who have a financial plan say they're living comfortably, and only 46% of households earning over $100,000 per year without a plan say the same.

So, in terms of living a comfortable lifestyle, having a written financial plan is as important if not more important than moving up the income ladder.

Non-planners who don't document their goals and keep them

top of mind often overspend and underinvest; when it's too late to achieve their dreams, they end up asking themselves, "Where did the time go? Where did all of *my money* go?"

But you're not going to let this happen to you.

How to document your goals in a life policy clarifier

Your goals should be expressed both numerically and in terms of what you want out of life. For example: *Save $250,000 for a second home in the greater Orlando area to play golf year-round and have the grandkids visit during winter break.*

Documenting your goals this way—so that they reflect your definition of wealth—will be a far greater motivator than just noting the dollar amount you'll need. In addition, by documenting them in this manner, if your target date for a goal approaches and it looks like you're not going to have the money to (as in this example) buy a second house, through creative financial problem-solving you may be able to achieve what you're really after—more golf and quality time with the grandkids—without buying the second home.

We'll cover this topic in greater detail in the next chapter.

How to score yourself on the life policy clarifier section of the scorecard

This makes up 3% of your total score, so you're going to grade yourself on a scale of 1–10, then multiply that grade by 0.3. A perfect grade of 10 gives you five points toward your total score.

Use the following scale to grade yourself:

Perfect 10: You have an up-to-date written financial plan that includes your top five to ten lifestyle goals. You have a good estimate of what each of those goals will cost you in the future. And your written financial plan is easy for you to find and reference so that you're regularly reminded of what you need to do to achieve true wealth.

Good 7.5: You've done a financial plan in the past, so you've gone through the process of documenting your goals. However, the document may not be up-to-date with your latest thinking, and the numbers need to be revisited for a reality check.

Average 5: You know what you want to achieve and have a good idea of what it will cost. However, the goals you've set for yourself have not been consolidated into a single plan for easy reference. Since you haven't "put it all together," you don't have a clear understanding of how realistic your goals are or what tradeoffs you may need to make.

Poor 2.5: You've been so focused on other areas of life that you haven't been able to put much thought into financial planning. If you've thought about your goals and maybe crunched some numbers on a spreadsheet here and there (but now don't know where to find it!), then this may be a good score for you.

Zero: You neither have a financial plan nor have you done any soul searching to determine what goals you would include in it. If this sounds like you, just give yourself a goose egg on this one and move on to the next category!

Liquid Purpose Fund: Do You Have Enough Cash Set Aside for Unplanned Expenses or Emergencies?

If you do not have a liquid purpose fund, you may have to sell assets at fire-sale prices in the event of an emergency. The liquid purpose fund is an account you put money into that is earmarked specifically for emergencies. This can be a savings or checking account, and in some cases, a home equity line of credit or even a CD that does not have early withdrawal penalties.

Financial emergencies can come in the form of a job loss, significant medical expenses, home or auto repairs, or something you have never dreamed of. The financially smart way to handle these emergencies is to have cash already saved—in a liquid purpose fund—to pay the bills.

How much do you need to have in your emergency fund?

Most experts agree that you should keep anywhere from three to twelve months' (depending on your specific situation) worth of your living expenses set aside in your emergency fund. As noted above, it is important to keep your emergency fund in a place that will be fairly liquid so that you can get to the money quickly in the event of an emergency.

How to score yourself on the liquid purpose fund section of the scorecard

This is only 2% of your total score, because the fix for a low score is relatively simple; and if you're strong in other areas, you can find additional ways to pay for emergencies—even though the alternatives to cash can be less than optimal.

Use the following scale to grade yourself:

Perfect 10: You have twelve months of living expenses in a highly liquid account or six months of living expenses if you perceive your income to be highly stable.

Good 7.5: You have three to six months of living expenses in cash or cash equivalent assets, and your income is relatively stable. A large expense or sudden loss of income would be uncomfortable but manageable.

Average 5: You have approximately three months of living expenses in cash, but an emergency greater than that or extended loss of income would force you to sell assets you planned to use for retirement.

Poor 2.5: You have the resources to pay for a financial emergency, but you have no assets that are not liquid. A high-cost emergency may force you to take an early withdrawal penalty from an IRA or 401(k).

Zero: A high-cost emergency or sudden loss of income would send you into an immediate financial tailspin: exorbitant credit card debt, inability to pay your bills, or even bankruptcy.

Income Capability: Are You Maximizing and Protecting Your Income-Producing Assets?

Over the years, businesses have learned that cost cutting goes only so far . . . sooner or later a company needs to grow to be successful. This lesson applies to individuals and families as well.

Containing expenses is important, but the ability to achieve your goals and sustain the lifestyle that makes you happy depends on your income capability. Income capability is defined as your ability to produce streams of income you won't outlive. Your income may come from many sources: wages, income from your own business, capital gains, dividends, Social Security, pensions, and so on. This category is critical to your financial independence, so its weighting is 15% of your total score:

- Contribution or withdrawal realities (10%)

- Social Security and pensions (5%)

You may not be able to score yourself accurately on this category until you've read chapter five, which focuses entirely on income capability. However, you can probably give yourself a ballpark preliminary score using the following guidelines for each subcategory.

Contribution or withdrawal realities (10%)

If you're in the wealth accumulation phase of preretirement, score yourself based on your contribution rate toward your retirement.

Perfect 10: You've been saving and investing 15% or more for your entire working career.

Good 7.5: You are saving and investing 15% or more now, but playing catch up from lower savings earlier in your career.

Average 5: You have 10% savings and investments.

Poor 2.5: You have 5% savings and investments.

Zero: You're far behind and haven't been saving consistently.

Keep in mind, there are many, many factors that go into whether you're contributing enough to your retirement savings: expected returns and risk profile, the size of your current portfolio, your income level, and your lifestyle needs, to name a few. Use the above scoring as a guide for now, and we'll dig deeper into income capability in chapter five. Ultimately, you want to be on a sustainable path to achieve financial freedom and your definition of wealth. For almost everyone, that means you're paying yourself first by prioritizing your own savings and long-term investments over discretionary spending.

If you're already retired, then what you're measuring is your withdrawal rate from your portfolio. The age-old rule of thumb is that you shouldn't spend more than 4% of your portfolio in any given year in retirement.

Retirees can use the following general guidelines to calculate their score for this subcategory, but keep in mind you can tweak your score up or down by considering the context of your other sources of income and how important it is for you to leave an inheritance to your loved ones:

Perfect 10: You have a 4% withdrawal rate (or less).
Good 7.5: You have a 5% withdrawal rate.
Average 5: You have a 6% withdrawal rate.
Poor 2.5: You have a 7% withdrawal rate.
Zero: Your withdrawal rate is 8% or higher.

Social Security and pensions (5%)

Certainty is a beautiful thing, especially when it comes to guaranteed retirement income streams. That's why Social Security and pensions make it onto the scorecard.

Because these two items are generally beyond your control, I won't spend too much time discussing them here, as you probably will not be able to move the needle much. Most employers do not offer pensions, and while Social Security is an underrated benefit from a financial point of view, it's generally a defined benefit (with many options).

What's important is that you don't leave money on the table.

Make sure you do your research on Social Security before claiming it. In addition, pay a professional to go through your options with you. Spending a few hundred bucks for quality advice is nothing compared to the certainty of knowing you made the right choices and potentially adding hundreds of thousands of dollars to your total lifetime benefit. Yes, claiming the right way and at the right time can add that much lifetime value.

To calculate your score on this subcategory of income capability, grade yourself from 1 to 10, then multiply by 0.5 (since this category is 5% of your total scorecard). Below is the scoring method with three benchmarks to use. (If you fall somewhere in the middle of the benchmarks, just use an average of the benchmarks you fall between):

Perfect 10: You've discussed your Social Security options in depth with an advisor, and your combined income from Social Security and pensions will cover both your fixed expenses and your leisure. This is the ideal scenario, but practically nobody gets a perfect 10 on this one these days, so don't feel bad!

Average 5: Your guaranteed income streams cover the basic necessities such as property taxes and utilities, but not much more. You haven't discussed Social Security with an advisor yet, but you haven't claimed yet either.

Zero: You have no pension, and your earnings history is too low to produce significant Social Security income.

Income Protection: Are Your Income and Assets Safe?

Your income-generating assets may be the lifeblood of your financial independence. However, achieving a comfortable lifestyle is only part of the game. In order to sustain that lifestyle with any degree of certainty, it's just as important to protect those assets.

Medical emergencies, prolonged illness, disease, premature death, injuries, and even lawsuits have the potential to derail a household's lifestyle. These are unpleasant events to think about, but addressing these risks may be the difference between a successful retirement and a story of regret. Shoring up these risks often helps families sleep easier at night, knowing their lifestyles and families are well protected.

For this reason, Income Protection is nearly one-fifth of your total score (17%). Here's the breakdown:

- Life Insurance & Disability Insurance (3%)

- Healthcare Strategy (6%)

- Personal Liability Insurance (3%)

- Long-Term Care (5%)

Life Insurance and Disability Insurance

This subcategory is all about income replacement in the unfortunate event of premature death or disability. Your life insurance benefit (plus your current investible assets) should ideally be the lesser of your current income multiplied by twenty-five, or your expected income between now and retirement. Keep in mind, however, that if your spouse and dependents are financially independent without your income, you don't need life insurance.

If you are unable to work, will your disability insurance payments be able to cover at minimum your monthly living expenses? Check employer-provided coverage and verify that it's sufficient.

If you have sufficient coverage in both of these areas to ensure lifestyle continuity through death or disability, give yourself a 10 in this category. If you are underinsured in only one area, your score is a 5. Of course, if your family's lifestyle is at risk in either scenario, your score is 0. The multiplier is 0.3.

Health Insurance

Will your insurance cover major medical expenses for you, your spouse, and your dependents? If you are retired, have you selected the Medicare option that will prevent you from draining your family's financial resources in the event of a major medical emergency or prolonged illness?

This category can be extremely complex and could be its own book, so I recommend reviewing your options with a specialist to determine your overall security or vulnerability in this area. Multiply your 1–10 score in this category by 0.6.

Liability Insurance (3%)

In today's litigious society, a lawsuit or similar claim can wipe you out, even if you're not really at fault. The court system isn't perfect.

Your liability insurance should cover your total assets so that a single incident doesn't hurt your income capability and derail your lifestyle.

In scoring here, give yourself a score from 1 to 10 and then multiply by 0.3. If your liability insurance covers 100% of your assets, give yourself a 10, an 8 if your insurance covers 80% of your assets, and so on.

Long-Term Care Planning:
Avoid Being a Burden to Your Loved Ones

According to the Department of Health and Human Services, 70% of Americans age sixty-five and older will need long-term care at some point in their lives. The cost of long-term care annually can range between mid-five figures and well into six figures, depending on your condition and where you live.

This type of event can absolutely derail your financial lifestyle, and it often comes down hardest on your closest family. Your spouse can be forced to accept a lesser lifestyle, your children's legacy may be spent on your medical bills, and you may face a situation where you either run out of money or have to ask family for help.

I've found that this is an emotional topic for aging retirees. None of us wants to become a burden to our loved ones. We want to age with dignity.

This is 5% of your score, so take your grade based on the guidelines below and multiply by 0.5:

Perfect 10: You have sufficient long-term care coverage.

Average 5: You don't have long-term care coverage, but you have a backup plan in place such as cash reserves or a facility in mind that you know you'll be able to afford. If leaving a legacy is important, you have some assurance (possibly life insurance) that your savings won't be wiped out.

Zero: The need for long-term care could wipe your family out financially

Lifestyle Preservation Enhancer: Avoid the Mistakes That Can Derail Your Lifestyle

Income capability is how you achieve financial independence. The Lifestyle Preservation Enhancer is how you sustain it for the rest of your life. That's why this category has the highest weighting on the scorecard, making up 30% of your score.

The subcategories of the Lifestyle Preservation Enhancer are some of the areas of personal finance where many people firmly believe they are doing the right thing, when in fact they are shooting themselves in the foot and hurting their own financial independence. The primary culprit for people losing their financial independence, in my experience, is *poor return on behavior*.

So, what is return on behavior?

According to a study conducted by DALBAR,[3] the average annu-

---

3   "DALBAR's 22nd Annual Quantitative Analysis of Investor Behavior," DALBAR, 2016, http://www.qidllc.com /wp-content/uploads/2016/02/2016-Dalbar-QAIB-Report.pdf.

alized returns of the S&P 500 index was 9.85% over a twenty-year period, while the *average equity investor* earned less than 5.19% during the same timeframe. The main reasons for this disparity between market performance and investor performance include

1. investors jumping in and out of the market at the wrong times based on fear and greed;

2. excessive portfolio volatility (poor asset allocation) that causes the underlying fear and greed; and

3. misguided market-timing strategies that dominate main-stream financial media.

Return on behavior and investor psychology will be covered in detail in its own dedicated chapter later in the book. In the meantime, you can grade yourself for the Lifestyle Preservation Enhancer section of the scorecard across the following categories:

- Return on Behavior (10%)

- Investment Policy Statement (5%)

- Asset Allocation (7.5%)

- Guaranteed Income (7.5%)

Use the following general guidelines to give yourself a preliminary grade on the Lifestyle Preservation Enhancer section of the scorecard, keeping in mind that you'll learn more about each topic later in the book when you can give yourself a more accurate assessment. Even after reading this book, I recommend speaking with a Certified Financial Planner before taking action.

How to score your return on behavior

Grade yourself from 1 to 10, based on how closely your actual behavior mirrors the following statement:

"I (or my advisor) reassess my portfolio strategy one to four times per year using an evidence-based process. I tweak my portfolio accordingly by reducing my investments in assets identified as overvalued and increasing my investment in assets that are undervalued. The risk level of my investment strategy remains consistent despite market volatility; I do not get more aggressive after market upswings, nor do I get more conservative during downturns. I consider the tax consequences of my buy-sell decisions."

Perfect 10: Your actual behavior as an investor mirrors this statement.

Good 7.5: This statement reflects your investing strategy, but you could do a better job of monitoring how your buy-sell decisions impact taxes.

Average 5: Your investing strategy remains consistent despite volatility, but you are not getting professional help or don't reassess your portfolio strategy often enough.

Poor 2.5: You mostly follow this advice, except when the market seems to be performing really poorly, when you sell to cut your losses.

Zero: You always try to time the ups and downs of the market to buy low and sell high.

Investment policy statement (5%)

An investment policy statement (IPS) describes the investment philosophies and procedures that will be used to help achieve your long-term goals. This helps guide your decision-making and avoid negative return on behavior. Grade yourself using the guidelines below, and then multiply by 0.5:

Perfect 10: You have a written IPS and follow it.

Average 5: You have a strategy that you follow, but it's not clarified in a written document.

Zero: You don't have a strategy. You simply pick the mutual funds that have performed well in the past and get stock tips from financial media and friends.

Asset allocation (7.5%)

Based on a study by the CFA Institute,[4] asset allocation—not the performance of individual investments—explains on average 93.6% of a portfolio's total returns. By "asset classes" I'm referring to categories of investments, usually available as exchange-traded funds (ETFs), such as large-cap growth (large market capitalization) or emerging market bonds.

This may be a difficult area to grade yourself without help from an advisor, so as a placeholder I would use the following benchmarks to get your grade. As with the other categories, when you fall in between the benchmarks, simply use an average:

Perfect 10: You're reviewed your asset allocation strategy within the past twelve months with an advisor you trust, and your advisor explained an evidence-based reason for why you're invested in the asset classes you're invested in.

Average 5: You've read a lot about investing and asset allocation, and you're confident you have a solid investing strategy. However, you haven't reviewed what you're doing with a professional investment advisor.

Zero: You invest in individual stocks and bonds, but you don't know how your investments are allocated across asset classes.

---

4   Gary P. Brinson, L. Randolph Hood, and Gilbert L Beebower, "Determinants of Portfolio Performance," *Financial Analysts Journal* 42, no. 4 (1986), https://www.cfainstitute.org/learning/products/publications/faj/Pages/faj.v42.n4.39.aspx.

Guaranteed income (7.5%)

Imagine someone offered you $10,000, and all you had to do to get the money was walk the length of a wooden board without falling. Picture that wooden board resting on the ground. It's a no-brainer to go after the $10,000, right?

Now imagine the wooden board you must walk across is suspended twenty feet in the air, and a fall has the potential to cripple you. Going after the money now is dangerous. Even if you think the board is wide enough for you to make it across, you're probably hesitating. I know I would!

Likewise, guaranteed income streams make it easier, emotionally, to stick with an investment strategy and avoid negative return on behavior that can derail your lifestyle. This is especially true during times of fear and greed, when you'll be tempted to abandon your strategy, and even truer when that guaranteed income stream can pay for a big portion of your lifestyle expenses.

It's also healthier to be able to sleep at night.

This doesn't mean that the more certainty you have, the better off you are. In the world of investments, you pay for certainty. Someone else is taking on the risk that you don't want, and they need to be compensated for that. So, you need to find the right balance between the level of certainty that you need to feel comfortable and the risk you can take in exchange for greater upside and long-term portfolio growth. Almost everyone needs growth to offset the ravages of rising prices.

Here's how to grade whether you have a healthy level of guaranteed income (multiply your grade by 0.75):

Perfect 10: Your guaranteed income exceeds the cost of your entire lifestyle, from necessities to recreation. You don't mind getting lower returns on your overall portfolio because you (or your advisor) have done the math and are confident you'll be able to sustain your lifestyle despite the rising cost of living.

Good 7.5: Either your guaranteed income exceeds your lifestyle needs and you would trade some of your certainty for higher expected returns, or your guaranteed income falls a bit short and you feel overexposed to the stock market's volatility. Either way, however, your guaranteed income will pay for necessities.

Average 5: Your guaranteed income can pay for necessities, or come close, but you're not confident that you can sustain your lifestyle as the cost of living rises.

Poor 2.5: Your guaranteed income covers part of your necessities, but you're stressed about the direction of the market. You fear a market crash will cause you to accept a less comfortable lifestyle than you want for yourself.

Zero: Your guaranteed income is insufficient. You find it hard to sleep at night because you're worried about a recession or crash in the stock market.

Income Tax Minimizer:
Are You Sending More of Your Money Than Required on a One-Way Trip to Washington, DC?

There's a saying, "It's not what you earn—it's what you keep that counts!" I've met with thousands of families during my career, and I've found that there is almost always room for improvement when it comes to your income tax expenses. If you earn more than you spend, you can probably reduce your tax bill by putting more of your money in the right types of accounts.

At 10% of your scorecard, here's how to grade yourself on this measure:

Perfect 10: You have a CPA do your taxes, and you invest the maximum in tax-deferred accounts such as a 401(k), traditional IRA, or 529 college savings plan. Your advisor implements loss-harvesting strategies and balances withdrawals between retirement and non-retirement accounts. Your advisor is in regular communication with your accountant for this reason.

Average 5: You invest in tax-deferred accounts but don't actively manage your tax bracket. You file your taxes using an online software program.

Zero: All of your investments are in non-tax-deferred accounts. You buy and sell securities for short-term gains, and don't implement any end-of-year loss harvesting tactics.

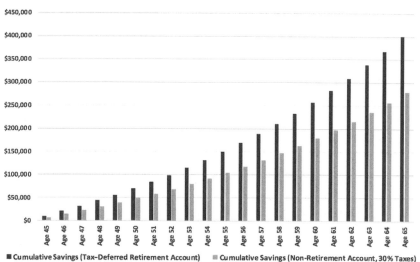

Portfolio Growth: Tax-Deferred Retirement Account vs. Non-Retirement Account

■ Cumulative Savings (Tax-Deferred Retirement Account)   ■ Cumulative Savings (Non-Retirement Account, 30% Taxes)

Legacy Assurance: Are Your Documents Up-to-Date?

The goal of leaving a legacy for your loved ones is common, but it's also very subjective. Some people want to leave behind everything they have and want to see the value of their portfolio remain constant throughout retirement for that reason. Others would like to spend their last penny on their final day on earth.

Wherever you stand on this spectrum, you definitely want your assets to make it to the people or organizations you care about if something happens to you. This category of the scorecard may not contribute to your financial independence, but it can give you peace of mind once you've taken care of it.

Worth 18 points on the Sustainability Scorecard in total, this category is divided into two sections: legacy assurance (8%) and documents, titling, or beneficiaries (10%).

Here's how to grade yourself on legacy assurance (multiply your grade by 0.8):

Perfect 10: You have a formal estate plan in place and a professionally written financial plan that prioritizes leaving a legacy to the degree you are comfortable.

Average 5: You have enough money to retire comfortably and remain comfortably retired. However, without a financial plan in place, you don't know exactly where to put your money or what your spending speed limit is to avoid putting the legacy at risk.

Zero: You don't have enough money to pay for your own retirement *and* leave a legacy.

To calculate your score on the documents, titling, and beneficiaries subcategory, give yourself a perfect 10 if all of your estate planning documents are up-to-date, including

- Will
- Health care proxy
- Power of attorney
- Trust
- Executor
- Beneficiary forms in investment accounts

Adjust your score down two points for each item you're missing.

Debt Management: Are Your Financial Obligations Restricting Your Financial Freedom?

As I mentioned in chapter one, freedom is a big component of true wealth. Fixed expenses in the form of debt obligations restrict your freedom and make it harder to achieve peace of mind. There are a million other things you would prefer spending your money on than bills.

Not all debt is bad. In many instances, I'll advise a client to keep some debt, such as a mortgage payment where the interest is tax deductible, as opposed to paying it off in full, especially when the interest is lower than the expected returns from your portfolio.

That's why this category is about debt management, not debt minimization. Use the following guidelines to assess how well you're managing debt. Multiply your score by 0.5.

Perfect 10: You are debt free or close to debt free. Your financial obligations have little to no impact on your peace of mind.

Average 5: You still have a mortgage and possibly some other debts (credit cards, student loans, etc.,), but you're on pace to have all debt paid off by the date you plan to achieve full financial independence.

Zero: You have excessive credit card debt that cannot be paid off within a month or two. The interest on your loans and debts is higher than the returns you're getting from your portfolio.

Next Steps . . .

Now that you have your Score, how did you do?

As I mentioned, most people get between a 40 and a 60 on their first assessment. With guidance from an advisor, almost everyone can get into that 85 to 95 range. Now that you have identified your financial vulnerabilities, the following chapters will help you address them in your pursuit of financial freedom, wealth, and peace of mind.

What's Most Important to *You?*

"Obstacles are what you see when you

take your eyes off of the goal."

—VINCE LOMBARDI

IN CHAPTER ONE, I wrote at some length about setting goals and how the type of wealth accumulation Wall Street encourages may not be suitable for the kind of lifestyle you want to lead once you reach retirement. In this chapter, I want to explain in more detail the importance of setting goals and making financial plans that can help you and those you care about live comfortably in your future years.

As a Certified Financial Planner, my first question to you as a client would be, "What's most important to you?"

Once you answer that question, you can start building a path that fulfills your needs.

In the retirement-planning business, there is a debate between financial advisors who support two different planning strategies:

cash flow–based planning and goals-based planning. I'm in favor of goals-based planning, but in order to show why, I need to explain how each method works.

Advisors who use a cash flow method create financial plans for their clients by analyzing likely circumstances in the future and determining which situation has the highest probability of coming true. With only one future scenario to account for, the advisor can recommend specific moves that will provide the cash flow needed to fulfill your financial needs in that future. Why don't I like this method? I'm not a fortune-teller. I want your financial needs to be covered whether or not the most probable future comes true.

In the past, the cash flow method for future planning may have been adequate for many families. Workers could count on their pensions for basic expenses, and the financial markets offered relatively favorable returns that would provide enough cash for a wide range of goals.

Unfortunately, this is no longer the case for many people in the United States, and taking a holistic approach can cause people to fall short of important future needs. I've found that goals-based planning improves my clients' chances of reaching a financial situation that accounts for everything from college tuitions to fitness memberships.

Setting goals works because it gives people a very clear picture of how much money they'll need in the future. With the cash flow method, it's easy to miss things like leaving a reasonable nest egg for the kids or having enough for potential medical expenses when you get older. If someone is undersaving using the goals-based method, it will be abundantly clear. As a financial planner, taking the guesswork out of saving and investing is one of the biggest gifts I can give to a family.

One of my favorite parts of goals-based planning is its ability to stir people's greatest passions. When I set out a plan that leads to a beach condo for ocean lovers or a life full of hitting the links for golf enthusiasts, I see the excitement in people's faces. When you have goals you're eager to reach, you'll be much more likely to reduce current spending when needed and follow the optimal savings and investment strategy. Not being able to afford the car you want in the future may convince you to eat out less or reduce your credit card debt.

Any system that gets you thinking about how your current spending and saving affect your future is good, and I think goals-based planning does this the most effectively. While seeing the big picture is important, specific goals give you the visibility and flexibility required to make changes when necessary. Deciding whether you're being too risky or conservative when you know the exact timeline for a financial goal is much easier than determining if a holistic strategy is working.

A Story about Goals-Based Planning

David and Susan were a couple in their early fifties, with two children nearing college, who came to me for investment advice. David earned a solid six-figure income as a lawyer and Susan volunteered at an elementary school. While the couple was proud to have only a small amount of household and credit card debt left, they enjoyed a lifestyle full of expensive dinners, theater performances, and luxurious vacations. In the future, they wanted to pay their kids' college tuition, maintain their comfortable lifestyle, take a trip around the world, and leave enough money behind to make their kids' lives a little easier.

I could have recommended that David and Susan lump all their future liabilities together and devise a holistic investment strategy, but as I discussed earlier, goals-based planning provides a much clearer path toward the future. By asking, "How much money do you need?" and "When do you need it?" for each goal, we were able to create six different goal-based strategies. When David and Susan saw how much money and time were required for certain goals, they were able to make realistic changes to their plan.

In our discussion about setting goals, David and Susan were forced to encounter a topic that's difficult for many people to talk about: What happens in case of the unexpected? Since David was the sole income earner in the family, we also needed to set some goals that accounted for Susan's and the kids' welfare if David were no longer able to earn.

How to establish goals

I have worked with clients in many types of similar situations over the years, but no two goal-based plans have ever been the same. Ultimately, no financial advisor can create a plan for you on their own. As a professional, however, I can give you valuable tips to help transform your needs and desires into tangible financial goals. I've listed out some general ideas that anyone trying to clarify their life policy should consider:

- **Plan as soon as possible.** If you've ever waited until the last minute to work on a school project or work assignment, you know the stress and confusion deadlines can create. By planning early, you can think rationally about a goal and make changes before it's too late.

- **Quantify your goals.** Generic goals like saving enough for college or living a comfortable retirement aren't very useful.

Setting a goal that can be accurately measured in financial terms means you'll know exactly what you need to do to reach it. You're much more likely to fall short when trying to fulfill abstract concepts.

- **Understand the effects of your decisions.** Whenever you create a goal, the financial means needed to reach it can affect your ability to meet other goals. Understanding how each decision has an effect on your entire financial outlook can help you create the right balance.

- **Planning is not fantasizing.** It's important to consider the reality of the world around you when planning. Unexpected events are a normal part of life, and they can affect your goals in drastic ways. Future financial security is not magic, and it requires realistic expectations about the markets and your own income.

To make things a bit more clear, let me walk you through the goals of two previous clients: Mr. and Mrs. Bobby Williams (I consider a married couple to be one client because they are a team working together) and Mary Jones. Mary came to me wanting to provide a legacy for her son, David, and to avoid being a burden on her loved ones. In the short term, my job was to help Mary quantify those long-term goals and make sure they were realistic. With an expected income of around $120,000, minimizing Mary's tax burden and maximizing earnings from her investments became important. We also needed to determine her income capability if she decided to retire or work on her own terms. I used her Lifestyle Sustainability Scorecard to identify, document, and shore up risks to these long-term objectives.

Mr. and Mrs. Bobby Williams came to me wanting to maintain a comfortable lifestyle through retirement while making sure that husband or wife would be okay financially in the event of the other's premature death. In order to reach these long-term goals, we needed to evaluate their income versus expenditures and their estate plan. Proactive, ongoing advice covering asset and income diversification, income tax planning, asset protection, and legacy planning were necessary to assure asset growth and income tax efficiency. Reducing the couple's chances of retirement ruin was also important.

In a world where people like Mary and the Williams family have a finite amount of money to work with, prioritizing goals is critical. I would love to tell a client with a limited income that they can travel the world, send their kids to college, and live in a beach house during retirement, but that may not be realistic. When discussing goals, I recommend that my clients make a distinction between desires and necessities. Deciding whether a goal is a want or a need can be difficult, especially for people who've had very comfortable lives; but I can help you prioritize with a few questions.

Let's start with, "Do I need to reach this goal to keep myself or someone I care about alive?"

Food, shelter, and medical expenses fall under this category, but only within reason. You need regular healthy meals, a well-maintained home or apartment with power and water, and regular health care; however, having a steak dinner every night isn't a need, and neither is having a large vacation home or cosmetic surgery. You may consider goals outside food, shelter, and health care very important, but being honest about which category they fall in can make life much easier in the future.

Once you create goals that satisfy your needs, you can ask, "What do I want most?" Goals within this category can range from "almost need" to "pure fun," and I try to get my clients to prioritize their wants based on the general well-being of their family. What may be very important to one person may be frivolous to another.

A few years ago, a responsible young couple named Mr. and Mrs. Brown came to me looking for financial advice. This couple raised two young children, earned a good living, loved to travel, and wanted to factor retirement and college savings into their financial outlook. My responsibility was to help the Browns set realistic goals to reach their desired future while allowing them to maintain a comfortable lifestyle in the present. To do this, I needed to evaluate what they wanted and needed in both the present and future.

While many Americans struggle to meet their financial needs without going into debt, the Browns managed to live comfortably without expenses exceeding their spending. Within the previous year, however, the couple took their young children on four expensive vacations while putting almost nothing toward an account for college. By creating a college savings goal, the Browns effectively made the decision to downsize their vacation budget. Many families opt to pay for college through student loans, but the Browns considered paying for college a priority over vacation fun.

Mr. and Mrs. Brown's retirement savings appeared to be higher than most couples their age, but without a measurable goal in mind, I wasn't sure if their short-term spending was properly balanced with their retirement expectations. By going through their needs and wants, we were able to set a list of realistic goals that allowed for travel and comfortable living conditions, without cutting into too much of their current living standards.

Are your assets aligned properly with your short- and long-term goals?

Once you create a list of goals you want to accomplish, it's time to start thinking strategy. Investing has huge effects on the lives of everyone in the modern economy, but ultimately it's a serious game. Winning this game requires the right timing, aggressiveness, and assessment of risk. All investments have a balance between risk and reward: Higher risk instruments tend to be more rewarding, and less risky investments are often less rewarding. When deciding what kind of investments you want to use for a specific goal, knowing the time horizon of that goal will be a crucial factor.

When planning your goal portfolio, you'll have the opportunity to take advantage of three different types of investments, each of which has its own risk-reward ratio. They are:

- **Cash investments.** This is money you have in a checking or savings account. There's little risk in losing this money, other than from inflation, but there's also almost no reward. Savings accounts at one time provided a very modest return, but federal policies have kept them close to zero for years. These can be useful to diversify for short-term goals.

- **Bonds.** Bonds are relatively stable financial instruments that increase with reward the longer you're willing to hold on to them. Treasury bills are considered one of the most trusted financial investments in the world. These are great for both short- and long-term goals.

- **Stocks.** Public stocks (or equities, as I call them) are sold in exchanges in many major cities around the world. The prices of company shares, some of which pay dividends, fluctuate due to a wide range of factors, including public opinion of said company, current market trends, crises around the world, and the buying and selling habits of other investors. Volatility of stocks makes them best for long-term goals.

The portfolio you create for each goal will likely contain at least one of every type of investment, but the percentage of money allocated to each tool will change as you shift from short- to long-term goals. Cash and bonds are relatively straightforward financial instruments with predictable futures, but the same can't be said for stocks. Mistakes two different families made during the financial crash of 2008 can help show you how stocks can be misused in both short- and long-term goals.

Mr. and Mrs. Johnson both graduated college in 2003, got great jobs in 2005, and then married in 2006. They knew investing for their future should be one of their top financial priorities, so they established several long-term goals for retirement, college, and some fun. As part of their long-term growth strategy, they invested a significant amount of money in the stock market. They invested mostly in high-tech enterprises and financial firms because they saw the most value in those industries.

In late 2007, the Johnsons noticed that their stocks were starting to lose value; but they knew this was a normal part of how the market worked, so they stuck with it. By September of 2008, however, the financial crisis was in full swing, and the market was losing as much as 5% per day. Investors everywhere were panicking, and the Johnsons were starting to worry about losing all their money. In November of 2008, they pulled nearly everything out of the market, losing nearly half their investment in stocks.

Because of this, it took a few years for the Johnsons to feel confident about putting money back into stocks. Unfortunately, they lost significant earnings by taking their money out near the bottom of the market. By pulling out and getting back in when they did, the Johnsons lost years of growth and opportunity.

Mr. Smith was in quite a different situation than the Johnsons during the 2008 financial crisis.

Just a few years away from retirement, Mr. Smith had a modest portfolio primarily made of bonds and cash. In early 2007, however, his daughter came to him asking for help with graduate school. By getting a master's degree, she believed she could increase earning potential for her family and help her father in retirement, if needed. Mr. Smith agreed, and he set a short-term financial goal of $120,000 to pay for his daughter's graduate program.

Unfortunately, Mr. Smith did not have nearly enough cash on hand to reach his daughter's goal within the short period of time in which she needed it. At the time, stocks were booming and most sectors of the economy were doing great, so Mr. Smith thought he would take advantage of the market and try to earn the money through aggressive investments. He took $30,000 out of a bond fund earning a slow-but-steady, single-digit annual return and put it into young companies he read were on the rise.

Investing in the stock market in the short term isn't a whole lot different than gambling; you will either be lucky or unlucky. When Mr. Smith put his money into the market in the summer of 2007, stocks were at a five-year peak. In the next year and a half, Mr. Smith lost 40% of his investment because of the crash. He took out what he could when his daughter's tuition came due, but a long-term or different short-term strategy would have suited her needs much better.

The lesson to be learned from these stories isn't about timing the stock market or even the risks involved with investing in equities. It's about aligning your assets with your short- and long-term goals. The Johnsons should not have sold off their equities during the market crash because they were very young and would not need income from those assets for several decades when they retired. Higher-risk investments with greater expected returns are often the most appropriate and best option for long-term lifestyle goals such as retirement. Had the Johnsons stood firm and kept their money in those investments, they would have recovered their losses within a few years and would actually be in better shape today relative to their long-term goals.

Mr. Smith, on the other hand, made the mistake of investing in those same higher-risk investments with greater expected returns to fund a short-term goal. That's when the volatility of the equities market can be really dangerous, and he got burned without the benefit of time being on his side. His assets weren't aligned with his goals, and he paid the price.

Unexpected events are a normal part of the stock market, but they are also a normal part of life.

When I talk with my clients about unforeseen personal calamities, they often get uncomfortable; but it's very important to discuss the possibility of needing additional financial assistance when bad things happen. This is why insurance is a crucial part of goals-based planning. Ideally, you should have just enough insurance to cover unexpected events without wasting money that could be earning more elsewhere.

As an example, long-term care can be the largest expense seniors face in their late years. While I don't expect all my clients to be placed in assisted living facilities, the costs of doing so can be enormous.

Medicare can cover a lot, but being underinsured for this long-term expense can eat away at your other goals. For clients in certain financial situations, I would consider any long-term care insurance as being overinsured, due to the earnings potential of their assets.

Once I help a client figure out if they have enough disability, life, health, or long-term care insurance, I want to discover if they are overinsured. Most insurance companies are for-profit businesses, so they're always looking for ways to improve revenue, even if that money isn't used to benefit clients. At a certain point, the additional money you spend on insurance will have diminishing returns. For example, many life insurance companies offer cash-value components that claim to earn you money over time. Putting that money in a stock, bond, or even savings account, however, may provide much higher earnings.

While insurance does offer some opportunities for wealth building, it is primarily used in goals-based planning for protection. In chapter six, the information provided can help you figure out what the right amount of insurance is by going into the details of each type of policy.

Keeping your goals on track

By now, you've probably thought of several different goals that you'd like to set for yourself and your family. While the general idea of each goal may be clear—save enough for college, own a vacation home, and so on—you may be concerned that you don't have the detailed information you need to reach it successfully. This is normal. Reading this book may be the first time you've ever thought about your future finances in any sort of detail, so you're unlikely to have the knowledge needed to create an on-track plan.

This is why seeking the advice of experts is so important. Financial planners like me have worked with people like you for decades. We've seen families set a wide range of goals, both ambitious and modest, and we've figured out what works and what doesn't. We can look at the nitty-gritty details of your income and spending to see where things are on track or off the rails.

By exploring topics, questions, and concerns that you are unlikely to think of yourself, you'll be able to clear the path of obstacles that have negatively impacted those who've come before you. You never want to repeat others' mistakes and move forward with a strategy that has proven over time to be too risky. In many situations, particularly retirement, this is your first and only chance to get it right. An advisor who has worked with hundreds of others in the same situation may clearly identify mistakes in your financial plan that seems logical and safe to you.

The type of expert you need will depend on the goals you have set. For example, if one of your goals is to split your relatively large estate evenly between your children when you die, you'll want to work with a professional estate planner. If avoiding as much taxes as possible is crucial to your comfort in retirement, you'll want to talk to a tax planner or accountant. Before you talk to an expert, make sure they have the required certification, education, or training needed for their area of expertise.

Once you have an established goal that's laid out in detail, figuring out if you're on pace to achieve it from time to time will be crucial. Doing so requires a detailed accounting of all your income, investments, expenses, and any other financial activities in your life. Whether you do this yourself with software or hire an accountant, a clear view of your finances will help you determine whether you have a shortfall or surplus. Earning too much money is a problem everyone wishes they had, but earning too little is an issue that requires an adjustment in strategy.

Let's analyze a hypothetical college savings goal you have for your only child who is currently ten years old. Based on research about tuition, housing costs, books, and other expenses, you've set a goal of $120,000 for four years of education with a time horizon of nine years. This goal's portfolio currently has $20,000 in assets. With planned contributions of $5,000 per year and a conservative growth rate of 4%, you figure out that you're falling about $13,000 short of your goal. One extra year and you'd reach your goal, but telling your child to wait an extra year may be the last thing you want to do.

When you encounter a shortfall, you need to ask yourself whether you're spending too much elsewhere, not implementing the right growth strategy, or simply not earning enough money in the first place. There's never a one-size-fits-all solution to any type of shortfall, so you'll need to examine every aspect of your financial life to see where there is room for improvement. My clients are often surprised how big a benefit can come from even the most modest changes.

If you're like most people, you're much more likely to encounter a shortfall than a surplus when examining your finances; but if you do have more money than you need for a certain goal, you have several different choices. Some of my clients use their surplus to better their current lifestyle. They go out to dinner more, go on nicer vacations, or they make home improvements. Other clients like to get more ambitious with their future goals. They plan a more comfortable retirement lifestyle, leave more for their children, or save for a really nice car they've always wanted.

Shortfalls may not be as fun to deal with as surpluses, but you're likely to find that there are plenty of workable solutions. If you're falling short of a long-term goal by a modest amount, you can get more aggressive with your stocks, or you can cut back on eating out and add the savings to your monthly contributions. If you're noticing large gaps, however, you may need to downsize or eliminate goals that are a lower priority. For example, you may need to cut back your future vacation budget in order to pay for long-term-care provisions.

I've found that most clients would rather increase their income or find ways to increase growth than make sacrifices in their current or future lifestyle. Increasing earnings through a better investment strategy can only take you so far, so I like to help my clients find ways to improve income from their careers or other sources. In the next few chapters, I will discuss in detail some of the ways you can increase your income capability and protect your income streams.

Maximizing Income Capability to Support Your Lifestyle Goals

"Risk is an inherent part of higher reward."

—HARRY MARKOWITZ

DO YOU KNOW what the most stressful part of retirement is for most people? It's the sudden absence of a weekly paycheck from your employer or the loss of steady profits from a business that you own. While you're still working and you're accumulating wealth, those bad days in the stock market are tempered by the fact that you know you have income from another source coming in to pay the bills and fund your lifestyle. You don't need to tap into your portfolio to live your lifestyle.

That all changes when you stop working. When those paychecks stop coming in, you'll be living off other sources of income: Social

Security, your pension (if you're lucky enough to have one), and income from your investments (including capital gains and dividends).

That's why your income capability is the foundation of your financial independence. Can you produce predictable streams of income that support your lifestyle for the rest of your life? As I mentioned in chapter three, on the Lifestyle Sustainability Scorecard your income capability generally has two components to it: how well you are producing enough income to sustain your lifestyle, and how well you are protecting those sources of income from the risks that may derail your lifestyle.

Remember, money is for security and peace of mind, and there is no universal, magical number for income that fits everyone. A lot depends on who you are as a person, and what you want out of life.

I have talked with people who are retired with only a modest amount of money, but they are very happy with their lives. I have also met very wealthy people who are not happy because they don't have financial peace of mind. There must be a balance between maximizing income and protecting that income so you can live without worry. We need to keep these truths in mind as we strive to generate enough income capability to support the goals we identified in chapter three.

It's also critical to prioritize your goals and organize them by the degree of necessity. What must you have? What would be nice to have? What could you live without if push came to shove and you had to make tradeoffs?

All of this goes into your overall income strategy, as your assets and the income streams they produce must be aligned with your goals. This is the path to true wealth.

What goals should you guarantee for yourself by purchasing certainty in the form of insurance or guaranteed income streams? What level of portfolio risk do you need to accept to achieve those goals that are nice to have?

The remainder of this chapter will take you through these questions and help guide you to develop an income strategy, customized for you and your family, that includes:

- Wages or salary

- Earnings from a business

- Investment income from your portfolio

- Social Security and/or pensions

- Protection from the risks that can undermine your income capability

Maximizing Lifetime Income

Unless you are in the very small minority of Americans who inherit great wealth, your salary or income from a business is the engine that drives your wealth accumulation. Nothing else really comes close. Sure, a penny saved is a penny earned, but you can't save what you don't have to begin with. That's why legendary investor Warren Buffet and many highly successful people say that investing in yourself is the best investment you can ever make.

As a financial advisor, I spend most of my time with clients advising them on what to do with their money after they've earned it. But I'll tell you this: I almost never discourage a client from investing in themselves to increase lifetime income or maximize the enterprise value of their business, even if it means they have less to invest in financial markets in the short term.

Take the example of an attorney who's a sole proprietor. He's forty-five years old, earning $200,000 per year, and saving $20,000 per year for retirement. He hits a wall, as many solopreneurs do, in not being able to grow his income without making improvements to his business's infrastructure. So he faces a decision: Keep his income where it is now, or make a $100,000 investment in the business, which will allow the attorney to hire staff in order to ramp up production and billable hours.

By increasing his income capability, he'll be able to improve his family's lifestyle with a higher income and also increase his annual investment contributions to $50,000 per year, starting in year two. If his projections are correct, the graph that follows shows the impact over a twenty-year period this has on his portfolio—assuming a 6% annual return.

Whether you are investing in a business or investing in your own education to get ahead in the corporate world, the math is the same (although you may have to adjust the numbers, based on the costs of the investment and the timeframe you expect it to pay off).

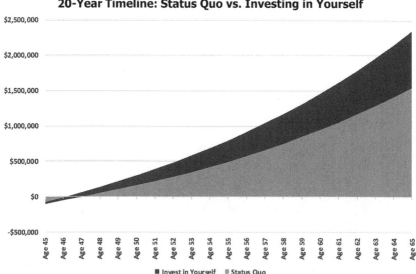

20-Year Timeline: Status Quo vs. Investing in Yourself

■ Invest in Yourself   ■ Status Quo

No matter your income, the same concept applies. Investing in yourself and being able to increase your annual earnings, whether it's as an employee or business owner, generally has the highest return on investment. All things being equal, the faster you can go from earning $50,000 per year to $75,000 per year, the better. The investment may be as substantial as getting an MBA or as small as picking up a book on how to use LinkedIn to get a higher-paying job.

I'll add a caveat to this wisdom of investing in yourself: Invest in yourself strategically and in line with your strengths.

In today's economy of specialization, you'll probably get more out of your investment by improving from *good* to *great* in one field than improving from *below average* to *average* in an area of weakness. Moreover, you should invest in yourself in a walk of life you're passionate about and where you'll have the energy to pursue greatness.

Here's an example of investing in yourself the wrong way: A friend of mine inherited a business from his father who had passed away. I was skeptical that this particular line of work was appropriate for him, so I suggested that he take a self-assessment test from a certified behavior analyst whom I have worked with for many years.

The test confirmed what I had suspected: Running this family business required the *opposite* personality type of my friend. Unfortunately, he went ahead and decided to take the reins as CEO anyway. He got burnt out from overwhelm—as the behavioral analyst had predicted—and the business failed.

There's a big difference between owning a business and running a business. A smarter investment *for him* may have been searching for a CEO to run the business while he continued to get income from the business's profits. He could either work in a smaller role within the company or enter a new field altogether. For *someone else* with the right skillset, taking over as CEO would be the right move. Self-awareness is important when deciding how to invest in yourself.

How baby boomers are redefining retirement

After years of consuming, many baby boomers either have a shortfall of assets or do not want to make the lifestyle compromises necessary to stretch their nest eggs for over thirty years. Instead of entering full retirement in a traditional way, millions of retirees are transitioning to retirement by working part-time or pursuing a second career with less stress. These second careers are usually more in line with their personal interests than professional ambitions.

A perfect example is a couple I know who built a lifetime of wonderful memories visiting Disney World with their children and grandchildren. When they retired, they took part-time jobs at Disney, which allowed them to get free tickets to the theme parks for the grandkids. The small amount of income they earned at Disney allowed them to afford meals out and bills for their RV, so they didn't have to feel guilty that they were spending their children's legacy as they partied in Orlando with Mickey, Donald, and the gang.

Both of their working careers were spent in public service, so they were certainly not rich in any traditional sense. But you'll never meet a happier couple—that's true wealth!

The point is you can define this period of your life in any way you like, and you don't have to go from a full income to zero income when you retire. Figure out how much you need, and be creative and open-minded when it comes to strategies that increase your lifetime income.

Maximizing Your Income from Your Investments

This is the stream of income that gets the most attention from financial advisors and the financial media—particularly when the topic is retirement planning. Sometimes we think of it as the main stream of income, and it can be—but it is just one stream.

A typical lifetime for an investor can be divided into two phases: wealth accumulation (when you're contributing to your accounts and growing your income capability), and income distribution (when you're withdrawing and spending your money, at a time when you're focused on protecting your income capability). Both phases have their own unique challenges and goals.

Growing your investment income capability during your working years

Your money should be working as hard for you as you did to earn that money. Every now and then, I'll meet someone whose entire savings is in cash—sometimes well over six figures of wealth, just sitting there—and the reason may be something like, "I don't trust the stock market."

It can be painful to see someone making this mistake. Depending on how long that money has been sitting idle in an account, they're not only failing to capture the long-term gains of the market—which has *always gone up over long timeframes*—but they're also allowing their money to be ravaged by the effects of rising prices and taxes.

The line graph that follows illustrates the effect of varying annual returns on a $500,000 portfolio during a ten-year period with annual inflation of 2.5%. The darkest line represents an average annualized 8% return, and the lightest line represents what happens to your $500,000 if you stuff it in a mattress. The math is the same for any size portfolio. (If you only have $50,000, simply take away a zero; if you have $5 million, congratulations, add a zero).

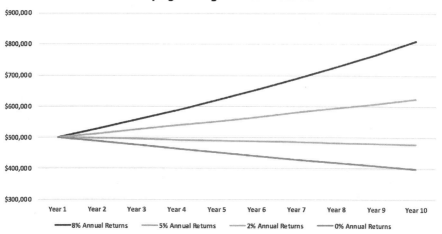

Not surprisingly, after adjusting for inflation the portfolio with an 8% return ends up being twice the value of the zero-return portfolio. Likewise, the 5% and 2% portfolios are in the middle.

Using the age-old rule of thumb that once you start withdrawing from your portfolio in retirement that you should spend no more than 4% of your portfolio value in a given year, here's the result this behavior has on your investment income capability:

Annual Investment Income Capability (4% Withdrawal Rate)

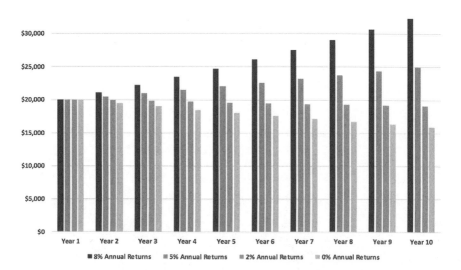

The portfolio that earned 8% returns grew to nearly $800,000 and safely produces more than $30,000 in annual income in the form of withdrawals, whereas the money stuffed in a mattress produces a little more than $15,000 annually. If your retirement lasts twenty years, the difference in total retirement income generated by your portfolio is $300,000. What would you do with an additional $300,000? That's the value of making your money work for you.

Avoiding Mistakes That Hurt Your Investment Income Capability

Most people do not make the mistake of earning zero interest. What happens, though, is that they jump in and out of the market at the wrong times, putting their returns somewhere in between 0% and the full gains of the investments they could have owned.

With markets more volatile than ever, the value of your portfolio can fluctuate quite a bit in a single day. Even in the good years, there's usually a single-day correction during the calendar year that sends shivers up and down the financial spine, temporarily reducing the value of the equities portion of your portfolios by 10% or more.

This is understandably unnerving for anyone who is either retired or approaching retirement. Nobody wants a stock market crash to derail their retirement plans. And that's where most investors go astray: By trying to avoid catastrophe, investors bail on the market and buy ultra-safe assets that will not produce the returns they need. Then they miss out on the rebound that has followed every crash.

This is called *bad return on behavior*, and I believe it's the most critical risk baby boomers face today.

Sometimes, doing nothing is the best course of action

Back in the day, in a year when the stock market had its worst start in history, I reminded nervous clients to ask themselves when they needed the money for lifestyle expenses. For most clients, they only needed between 4% and 6% of their total portfolio to live their life-styles for the entire year—that's between 1% and 1.5% for the first three months of the year! When you look at it that way, the stock market earthquake we experienced wasn't as threatening.

For those who were retired and needed withdrawals to fund their lifestyles, they took out the 1–1.5% from the conservative portion of the portfolio that didn't lose any money. This gave their more aggressive investments time to rebound and even grow, unaffected by the temporary market swing.

Clients who were still in the wealth-accumulation phase and did not need any money from their portfolio were encouraged to simply stay put. Sure enough, their portfolios soon recovered, and their income capability was preserved.

Social Security and Pensions

As employer-guaranteed pensions are becoming a relic of the past, Social Security has become a more integral part of Americans' retire-ment income plans. Before briefly discussing the value of Social Security and why I encourage clients to wait as long as possible to claim it, I want to address a very damaging yet common misconcep-tion: Social Security is not going away anytime soon. Yes, govern-ment budget deficits and ballooning debt are a problem. And yes, there is a projected shortfall. However, even pessimistic projections indicate that a worst-case scenario is that benefits will be *reduced*, not eliminated, by 15% or 20%. If you're reading this book as a baby boomer, Social Security will not be eliminated in your lifetime.

How valuable is Social Security?

This benefit is the guaranteed portion of your income that rises with the cost of living. If you wanted to replicate a guaranteed lifetime income stream that is on par with Social Security, one that is protected from market crashes as well as inflation, you would have to spend $500,000 or more to purchase an annuity in the private market.[5]

Also, don't make the mistake of assuming Social Security is a fixed benefit with no upside. Many retirees add well over six figures in lifetime income by claiming at the right time and in the right way. Talk to your financial advisor about your options in this area. There are things you can do in the years leading up to retirement to set yourself up well strategically so that you can delay claiming your benefit and add 8% *per year* to your monthly payout.

The Value of Guaranteed Income Streams

As you can tell, I'm a big believer in financial markets and their ability to improve investors' financial lives. However, I'll be the first to admit that markets aren't perfect. They don't always provide the level of certainty that some people need for peace of mind, effective planning, and risk taking. The more guaranteed income you have, the less stress you may feel, and the more comfort you'll have in taking on some necessary risks.

For most people, I advise them to wait as long as possible to claim Social Security. Waiting makes the monthly payments bigger when

---

5   This is based on the cost of an annuity that pays $2,639 monthly (the maximum Social Security benefit in 2017) and increases payouts at a rate of 2.5% per year for thirty years.

you do claim and increases your guaranteed inflation-protected income streams when you may need them most: as you get older and when markets tumble.

The same holds true for a pension. While the lump-sum option may be tempting and provide you with a lot of flexibility, especially in the short term, the payments-for-life option has its own benefits. It's easier to budget, easier to manage your investing behavior, and easier to avoid mistakes that may derail your lifestyle.

Below is a short case study of a rare couple where both had a pension. My firm advised them on how to take it and when to claim Social Security.

Balancing guaranteed income streams with flexibility

This couple enjoyed a rare circumstance where they both had pensions. Their chief financial worry was that the husband had health issues, and if he passed away, the wife would not get his pension payments. He had filed for a single benefit before coming to us, and this decision could not be reversed. This was income they were both relying on to live their lifestyles.

We advised her to take a lump-sum pension payout so she could roll that over into an IRA and have it continue to grow tax-deferred. The reason for this was that they were living comfortably without it, and the husband's Social Security and pension were sufficient in the meantime. Had she opted to receive pension payments, they would have been taxed as ordinary income—unnecessary, given that the couple didn't need the money at the moment. Why pay taxes on income you don't need yet?

In addition, by delaying her Social Security claim, her benefit grew at 8% per year. Allowing her lump-sum pension to grow in an investment account and increasing her Social Security benefit gave the couple peace of mind in knowing that the wife would have plenty of guaranteed income *and* financial flexibility if her husband died prematurely.

Protecting Your Income Capability from Critical Risks

Now that we have looked at the income streams, we need to make sure there are no threats that can destroy those streams. Risks that may derail your income capability include:

- Health care emergency

- Sudden loss of a job

- Death of an income-earning spouse

- Short- or long-term disability

- Exceeding your spending speed limit

When you're healthy and successful, it's easy to become overly optimistic. In fact, DALBAR's Quantitative Analysis of Investor Behavior identifies optimism as one of the nine behavioral mistakes investors make that hurt their returns.[6] This extends to other areas of personal finance as well.

I don't want to delve into the ins and outs of the insurance marketplace for life, health, and disability insurance, but I will say that if you

---

6   "DALBAR's 22nd Annual Quantitative Analysis of Investor Behavior," DALBAR, 2016, http://www.qidllc.com /wp-content/uploads/2016/02/2016--QAIB-Report.pdf.

haven't reviewed your protection in a while, it's likely you'll find areas where you're underinsured or exposed to these risks. I also recommend reaching out to a Certified Financial Planner who can help you determine whether you're overpaying for your current coverage.

With regard to exceeding your spending speed limit, outliving your money is a real risk for many people, even those who were once financially independent. Running out of money is a retiree's greatest fear (more so than death!).

This risk isn't only about what you do with your money after you retire. While you're working, if you can commit to saving 20% of your income for your entire working career and investing it in a disciplined way in a well-structured portfolio, without jumping in and out of the market, you will almost certainly have amassed a nest egg that can produce predictable streams of income that support the lifestyle you're accustomed to.

When you're on the other side of the fence, the withdrawal side, that's when spending discipline comes in. I recommend that you treat your accounts as your employer used to: Give yourself a monthly paycheck. Your employer didn't pay you more in a given month just because you wanted to buy something. Base your "salary" on how much you can afford to spend without the risk of running out of money—whether your advisor tells you it's 3.5%, 4%, or 6%—and stick with that amount.

It's Not What You Earn; It's What You Keep That Counts

Finally, but definitely not the least important, when looking to maximize your income capability, it's essential to focus on post-tax income. Money that you earn and send to the government in the form of taxes cannot give you financial freedom.

Income taxes are most households' greatest expense. While we cannot change the tax rates, we can control where we invest our money. This often has a major impact on how much of our hard-earned money we keep to support our lifestyles and secure our futures.

As a rule of thumb, if you earn more than you spend, you can likely reduce your tax bill by putting your income in the right types of accounts: 401(k), Traditional IRA, SEP IRA, and Roth IRA accounts are a few examples of places you may be able to reduce your tax burden by five figures annually. Later in this book, we'll dive deeper into this topic.

Protect your assets

Income is the foundation of your financial independence. Remember, though, it's not the endgame. It's only 25% of your Lifestyle Sustainability Score. After you earn the income, you still have to make wise decisions with it and make sure you protect it to the extent possible. The following chapter introduces strategies to preserve the lifestyle that your income affords you by investing the right way and developing a personal budget that works for you and your family.

Protecting Your Income from Catastrophic Risks

"Risk is like fire: If controlled it will help you;

if uncontrolled it will rise up and destroy you."

—THEODORE ROOSEVELT

JAMES THOUGHT HE had done everything right. He had worked hard all his life, put some money in the bank, paid down the mortgage on his home, and taken care of his children. After a lifetime of hard work and sacrifice, James could finally see the retirement light at the end of the tunnel.

Then, James's wife, Janet, began to experience strange health problems, from headaches and mood changes to issues with balance and mobility. After consulting dozens of specialists, James's and Janet's worst fears were confirmed. Janet was suffering from early-onset Parkinson's disease, and she would soon lose her ability to be safely left at home.

Suddenly, James had to make a decision—hire a full-time caregiver, wiping out his retirement funds, or take care of Janet himself, which would mean an early exit from his career and an equally devastating blow to his carefully preserved retirement funds.

We all know this could happen to us, but the danger never seems real until it actually happens. It is not enough to follow an "invest and hope" strategy when developing your financial plan. You need to plan not only for the sunny future you envision but also for the risks that can derail your lifestyle. Hopefully, no one in your family will suffer the catastrophic events James and Janet have had to endure, but it is critical to be prepared.

This chapter is dedicated to the income-protection category on the Lifestyle Sustainability Scorecard, which helps minimize the financial risks that commonly blindside people and completely wipe them out—either immediately or within a few years. The following pages will cover:

- How to protect your income from premature death or disability

- How to plan for the soaring costs of health care

- How to protect your assets from personal liabilities

- How to avoid going broke should you need long-term medical care

Protection against the Unthinkable: Premature Death or Disability

Unfortunately, I do not have any ideas about how to avoid death. It's also unavoidable that a certain percentage of my readers will suffer from a major accident that will require recovery time, and they will be unable to work. These events are undesirable in and of themselves for nonfinancial reasons. The potential impact on a family's finances can make a bad situation even worse.

Let's start the discussion by talking about life insurance. The first question is, "Do you need life insurance?" and then, if so, "How much and what kind?"

There may be some times in your life, like when you are young and unattached, that you truly do not need life insurance. Another example would be if you've amassed enough savings so that your surviving loved ones are able to continue their lifestyles and afford the things you want for them after you pass away. For most people, there are other times, like when you start a family and have young children who rely on you and your income, when life insurance coverage is vitally important.

How much life insurance do you need?

A common mistake people make in answering this question is to look at the life insurance benefit as a lump sum. It's actually a lot more practical to consider the income you will need to replace when an income-earning spouse passes away. After all, lifestyle expenses are incurred over time, and we generally pay for those expenses with our income, not out of a lump sum.

We will use $1 million as an example. This may sound like a lot of money and enough to support a surviving spouse. When you think about it as income, however, that million dollars translates to $40,000–$50,000 a year as a predictable lifelong income stream.

Is that enough? Maybe, maybe not.

What monthly expenses will the surviving family members have to pay? Are there any major expenses you know you'd like taken care of, such as a child's wedding or education? Ultimately, it comes down to what you and your spouse need taken care of to have financial peace of mind.

Next, assess the income capability of the surviving spouse. Does he or she have a reliable career and income stream of their own? Then look at the money being left behind by the deceased in the form of savings, investment accounts, and other assets. How much income can these assets produce?

Will these income streams cover the lifestyle expenses and other major financial objectives you feel are necessary for the peace of mind of both spouses? If not, you'll want to bridge that gap with life insurance.

Keep in mind, if that gap is too wide and the cost of insuring that amount is simply too high, the family should have a discussion about that. Maybe you don't insure the full amount and instead simply have a plan that you agree on, such as downsizing your house, the car, or some other aspect of your lifestyle that you're comfortable downsizing. These conversations aren't as much fun as going to a cocktail party or binge-watching a favorite TV show together, but couples who address these issues find the process rewarding. It eliminates lingering uncertainty that you may not even realize existed until you've addressed it.

Choosing the life insurance option that's right for you

Now that you know the size of the death benefit you'd like to leave behind, it's time to decide what type of life insurance to buy. Keep in mind, while life insurance is primarily considered a death benefit, it has many other uses that most people are not aware of—particularly when it comes to estate planning and leaving a legacy in a tax-efficient manner. However, since this chapter is about income protection, the focus here will be on replacing income for dependents if you die prematurely.

There are many different kinds of life insurance, each with its own unique set of benefits. The two I'll compare here are term life insurance versus whole life insurance (a type of "cash value" insurance that my firm often recommends to clients).

Let's say that Bill M., a successful manager at a major Fortune 500 corporation, is getting married. Suddenly, Bill M., who never even thought about buying life insurance, now has a new bride to protect. He takes out a term life insurance policy with a death benefit equal to ten times his annual $100,000 salary. That $1 million death benefit will help his grieving widow, who does not currently work outside the home, to regain her financial footing and eventually move on with her life.

As Bill M. and his new bride move through their lives, they welcome a new addition to their family. Suddenly Bill M. is a proud papa as well as a loving husband, and he has even more to protect. By the time his five-year term life policy expires, he has a toddler in the house and needs a more substantial death benefit.

Bill M. is now making $150,000 a year and he wants to up his death benefit to twenty times that amount. That means a $3 million term life insurance policy, and since Bill M. is now five years older, the premium price tag has risen substantially. Bill M. begins to shop around, looking not only at other term life policies but other types of insurance as well.

If Bill M. decides to purchase a whole life policy, he can combine the death benefit that protects his wife and child with an investment component that helps his family save for the future. In sixteen years, when his two-year-old toddler is looking at colleges, Bill M. can borrow against the cash value of his whole life policy to offset the cost of tuition and supplement college loans, grants, and other ways to pay for college. If his child gets a scholarship and the money is not needed for tuition, the value of the policy may be used for retirement income or any other lifestyle goals Bill M. and his family may have.

Term life insurance would be less expensive than whole life, but it has no savings component. Once the term ends, it's over and you don't get anything back. The downside of whole life insurance is that it's more expensive, and you run the risk of earning a smaller rate of return on the investment component of the insurance than you would have earned had you invested the money elsewhere.

Your final decision may come down to a few factors:

- Your tax situation, as there are many creative ways to use whole life insurance for estate planning, education planning, and other goals in a tax-efficient manner.

- Your risk profile as an investor; if you're of the mindset that you're willing to accept more risk in exchange for higher expected returns, you're probably better off with a term life insurance and investing the savings.

- The level of certainty vs. flexibility you want, as the more expensive whole life insurance gives you a more certain pay-out, while lower cost term insurance gives you more flexibility.

Because there is not one definitive right answer, this is a topic that I'd strongly recommend discussing with a Certified Financial Planner.

Protecting Your Income if You Become Unable to Work

Disability insurance is not the most exciting topic in the world, but it's on the Lifestyle Sustainability Scorecard for a reason: The inability to earn income due to a physical injury or mental health issue is a leading cause of extreme financial hardship in the United States.

Imagine the case of a successful self-employed attorney who was one of those people who always seemed on the fast track to success. After a stellar stint in college and an exceptional law school career that included interning for a state Supreme Court justice, she was able to build a solid client base, helping individuals and businesses stay on the right side of the law and avoid entanglements with Uncle Sam.

Everything was going great, until she was severely injured in a weekend boating accident. That accident left her incapacitated for months, unable to serve her clients or even keep the lights on in her office. Worse yet, she had a family to think about and a spouse currently pursuing his master's degree. With the bills piling up and nowhere to turn, this single event could turn her dream life into a nightmare. The right level of disability insurance, combined with a backup plan to keep the firm running in her absence, could have prevented her accident from essentially ruining her life.

Much like life insurance, the level of disability insurance you need varies based on your current level of coverage, your lifestyle expenses, and how much your loved ones rely on you for income. If you are working, your employer may provide a basic level of disability insurance, separated into short-term and long-term disability benefits.

If you're a business owner, the question becomes, "What will happen to the income you're currently generating from your business if you become disabled?" As a painter, your income may disappear.

If you've grown your business so that it can run itself without you physically being there, you may need a smaller level of insurance.

Your family's financial lifestyle is not truly secure unless it's protected from the hardship of disability. So, make sure you review your coverage to ensure lifestyle continuity.

Having a Health Care Strategy Is a Critical Component to Lifestyle Sustainability

A recent survey of actual retiree experiences is both eye-opening and frightening. That study found that the average lifetime health care premium costs for a sixty-five-year-old healthy couple retiring today is a staggering $266,589, and the cost rises to nearly $400,000 factoring in dental, vision, co-pays, and out-of-pocket costs.[7]

How will you pay for this? First, here's what *not* to do:

- *Don't* overlook health care costs when doing your cash flow analysis of how much income you'll need in retirement. This is a surefire way to undersave, underestimate how much money you'll need, and possibly end up running out of money.

- *Don't* simply opt for the health insurance plan that has the lowest premiums but leaves you vulnerable to financial devastation in a near-worst-case scenario.

- *Don't* make your health care decisions entirely on your own, especially when it comes to enrolling in Medicare at age sixty-five; an advisor who knows how to navigate the Medicare maze may prove to be invaluable.

---

7   http://www.lifehealthpro.com/2015/03/26/these-5-charts-predict-what-retirees-will-pay-for.

Instead:

- Choose your health care insurance carefully.

- Understand the various parts of the policy and how well they cover any expenses you may incur, particularly the costs of catastrophic care that could wipe out your finances.

- Whether you are comparing the benefits of your employer-sponsored coverage or shopping for health care insurance in retirement, you need to look at total out-of-pocket costs, percentage copays, and other potential expenses.

- Build all costs into your budgeting and retirement-planning strategy.

- Value predictability; paying an additional $1,000 a year is not as likely to derail your lifestyle as that 10% chance you get stuck with a $200,000 medical bill from one event.

Other than being as healthy as possible, there is really nothing any individual can do about soaring health care costs. What we can do is plan accordingly, save enough to pay for them, and avoid that one big mistake.

Choosing the Right Options for Medicare

Ever since its inception, Medicare was designed to offset the high cost of medical care for eligible seniors, and it does—up to a point. Medicare does indeed help seniors pay for their doctor visits, hospital stays, and required surgical procedures, but its benefits are limited and retirees may still incur significant out-of-pocket costs.

In addition, the premiums associated with Medicare and the supplements seniors are advised to get can really add up over time. Think back to the more than $266,000 the average retired couple is expected to spend over their lifetimes, and consider how those costs will likely impact your own retirement plans.

As with any health care coverage, it's important to not just default to the Medicare coverage with the lowest premiums. This would be a mistake that may cost you dearly. The cost of major medical care is so high that, even if your Medicare plan covers 80% of costs, the remaining 20% that you must pay could be a major blow to your lifestyle throughout retirement.

There are many options and ways to take Medicare. Many advisors within my industry refer to it as the *Medicare Maze*. It's so complicated, in fact, that the *Medicare for Dummies* book is 351 pages long!

I couldn't possibly go into full detail about this without it taking up nearly this entire book. For a more detailed look at Medicare, I'd recommend visiting my company's presentation on the subject.[8]

What Is Personal Liability Protection and Why Do I Need It?

Imagine you are having a backyard barbecue—just a couple of friends, a box of burgers, and some outdoor fun. You invite some friends from work, open your deck and patio to the neighbors, and start grilling. Your friends and neighbors are having a great time, at least until an errant flame erupts from the grill and burns off a

---

8   www.rebyadvisors.com/medicare-maze.

guest's eyebrows. You rush the victim to the hospital, the eyebrows are saved, and everyone has a good laugh.

The laughing stops when you receive a letter from the individual's lawyer, claiming loss of income, post-grilling stress, and punitive damages. If you have personal liability insurance, you can turn the case over to the firm's lawyers and rest assured that any judgment up to the amount you're insured for will be covered. If you lack such protection, you could find yourself on the hook for hundreds of thousands of dollars (or millions) in legal fees and other expenses.

Personal liability protection is very important and may even be part of the homeowners insurance you already carry. Keep in mind, however, that even if this is the case, you may need additional coverage, over and above the limit on your homeowners insurance. Umbrella coverage can provide a million or more dollars in personal liability protection and give you additional peace of mind the next time you light the grill and put on some burgers.

The cost of this additional protection is generally low, so talk to your agent about adding it to your policy. We live in a litigious society, and you never know when a simple injury or accident at your home will turn into a costly lawsuit. Many people have umbrella coverage, forget about it for a while, and as their wealth grows become underinsured.

With the low cost of this insurance, there's little reason to leave it up to chance. Review your current coverage and get more if you need it.

How to Protect Your Income from the Potentially Devastating Cost of Long-Term Care

I used to discuss longevity risk as one of the most serious risks that can jeopardize retirement. Longevity risk refers to the risk of living longer than expected and potentially outliving your money. I no longer discuss this risk, because I don't consider it a risk any more. With life expectancies continuing to rise, I just consider it a fact of financial planning that the couples I work with will have at least one spouse live well into their nineties.

While it's great that we're living longer these days, this also means our money has to last longer. And on top of that, the older we get, the more we're at risk to need long-term care at some point in our lives. In my home state of Connecticut, long-term care costs more than $100,000 per year.

You may still feel like a spring chicken and be far from the age where this may affect you personally; but keep in mind that inside every old man is a young man who can't believe how time flies.

The Financially Crippling Effect of Health Issues on the Elderly

We started this discussion with the harrowing tale of James and Janet, the soon-to-be-retired couple who thought they were doing everything right. We saw how the couple quickly learned that they were a single life-changing event away from financial ruin, and how one devastating illness could derail decades' worth of careful working, saving, and investing.

Unfortunately, the story told by James and Janet is far from unique, and there are plenty of other couples in the same precarious situation. A long-term illness or sudden accident is often the start of a sort of downward spiral—one that ends in bankruptcy and financial ruin.

The cost of long-term care can, and does, wipe people out, leaving them with a difficult choice between spending down their resources to qualify for help from Medicaid and spending the funds they have accumulated to pay for the care themselves.

Suddenly, the money they hoped to leave to their heirs or use to build a legacy is now tied up in the ever-increasing cost of nursing home care and other long-term care services. These costs are going nowhere but up, and if you have not made arrangements to protect yourself, your retirement planning is not complete. And even if retirement is ten or fifteen years away, that makes now an even better time to start preparing, either through traditional insurance, self-insurance, or even planning for another form of care.

If you are married, long-term care insurance can protect your spouse in the event you need nursing home services. If you fail to plan for this eventuality, your spouse could be left with a lesser lifestyle, struggling to make ends meet.

To illustrate this important point, consider the case of another couple, Glenn and Beth. Like James and Janet, Glenn and Beth have been doing everything they can to save for retirement, but unlike James and Janet, Glenn and Beth have already stopped working.

They are enjoying a wonderful lifestyle, traveling, visiting the grandkids, and even building their dream home right on the beach. They are living the American post-retirement dream, and things look great—until Glenn is left disabled, and his wife is left devastated, by a sudden stroke.

The once-vibrant Glenn is now confined to a wheelchair, struggling to do simple things like bathe, eat, and attend to his personal hygiene needs. His wife, Beth, struggles as well—at her advanced age, simply lifting Glenn out of his wheelchair leaves her gasping and out of breath.

Glenn and Beth realize that they cannot go on like this, so they start looking into nursing home care. They are surprised and appalled at the costs, which can easily exceed $10,000 a month. Even with the substantial resources they have built through a lifetime of hard work and financial dedication, they realize that the high cost of nursing home care will quickly wipe them out and leave them penniless.

Just like that, Glenn and Beth's dreams of passing their house and a nice sum of money on to their kids is gone. The house, along with all their other property, will either go to the nursing home directly or be liquidated so that they will eventually qualify for long-term care under Medicaid. This devastating and humiliating scenario is all too common. Instead of growing old with dignity in their own homes, these hardworking retirees must spend their last days, and their last dollars, in institutional nursing homes.

Hoping for the Best but Planning for the Worst

Fortunately, there is a way to avoid this all-too-common hardship. Long-term care insurance is designed to provide protection against just such a scenario, and its purchase should be an integral part of your retirement strategy. If you can't afford it, then you need a plan to at least mitigate the risk.

The bad news is that this insurance can be expensive. The good news is that it may be surprisingly affordable for men and women in their forties and fifties. While there may be some premium increases along the way, it makes sense to explore your options now and weigh the costs against the costs of waiting until you're older, when the premiums will be much higher.

It is important to know that the cost of long-term care is usually not covered by Medicare, and Medicaid only becomes an option after you've pretty much run out of money. So you need to assess the potential impact of those care needs on your family's income and financial objectives, because the burden will be on you and your family should the need arise.

What would you do if you needed long-term care tomorrow? How would you pay for it? Where would the money come from? How long could you pay? If you cannot answer these questions, you need to start researching long-term care insurance.

Reviewing Your Potential Long-Term Care Needs

As I mentioned, long-term care insurance can be expensive. Top-of-the-line insurance is not affordable for everyone, or even advisable if the financial burden of insurance is too great for you to enjoy your lifestyle. Here are a few options:

1. Insure for 24/7 care, in-home or in a nursing home.

2. Insure for assisted living, with some care in a facility.

3. Insure for part-time in-home care, with family members helping out the rest of the time.

Also consider the emotional cost of knowing you may become a burden to your loved ones. What impact will this have on your family? Will any family members even have the ability to take care of you?

These are the questions to really consider when assessing your need for this high-cost insurance product that has the potential to truly save your nest egg should you be unfortunate enough to need it.

Again, I realize this isn't the fun side of money and financial planning, but going through the reality check, answering these tough questions for you and your family, and deciding which route to take (even if that means accepting the risk of being underinsured) will almost definitely make you feel more confident in the path forward.

Long-Term Care Options to Consider: Asset-Based versus Traditional

One choice you'll face is deciding between asset-based and traditional insurance. Asset-based insurance requires a large lump-sum payment or a few installments. The advantage of asset-based insurance is that your cost is known upfront, and if you pass away before needing long-term care, your beneficiaries get some of that money back.

Traditional long-term care premiums are paid annually, until you need the benefit, making the cost unknown because you don't know how long you'll live. This is a disadvantage, because certainty is always a good thing for planning purposes. In this case, as long as you live, you continue paying the premiums. One advantage to this is that you do not have to tie up a large amount of money all at once.

Long-term care is a specialization within the field of financial planning, and to go through all options in detail would require a separate book. So I would recommend doing some research on your own and discussing some options with an advisor you trust.

Your Income Is Protected;
Now Preserve Your Lifestyle

As this chapter focused on the risks that can completely derail your retirement with a single one-time event, the next chapter details how to minimize the risks that damage your income capability over time. The danger in these lifestyle risks is that you don't see them coming, and rarely do you see an immediate impact.

However, these sneaky risks are more probable than the ones discussed in this chapter and every bit as dangerous to your lifestyle sustainability: return on behavior, rising prices and taxes, and your overall approach to spending and investing.

The Most Critical Financial Risk Facing Investors Today

BEHAVIORAL RISK

"The key to making money in stocks is not to get scared out of them."

—PETER LYNCH

CHAPTER THREE INTRODUCED the Lifestyle Sustainability Scorecard and a systematic process for minimizing the risks to your family's lifestyle, and chapters four and five covered two of the eight categories on the scorecard. Not all categories on the scorecard are equal. The Lifestyle Preservation Enhancer comprises 30% of an individual's score, as these are the financial risks that affect nearly everyone and are the most likely to derail your lifestyle: behavioral risk, outliving your assets, and your asset allocation strategy.

Because this category of the scorecard is so critical, it deserves three chapters. This chapter introduces behavioral risk and how to manage your return on behavior to achieve better long-term gains, and the following chapter will include additional financial planning advice on how to avoid outliving your assets. Then, we'll wrap up this section of the scorecard with a chapter on asset allocation, or how smart investors profit from evidence-centered investing.

Investors Recently Earned 8.19% Less Than Unmanaged Index—Why?

To avoid outliving your money, it's critical for your investment income to grow with rising prices and taxes.

Yet average equity fund investors—including people who seek professional financial advice—recently earned 8.19% less than the unmanaged S&P 500 over a twelve-month period.

Underperformance against unmanaged indices also holds up over longer timeframes, as investors earned average annual returns of only 5.19% compared with 9.85% for the S&P 500 during a twenty-year period.

To put that in perspective, average equity fund investors with $250,000 would have nearly $950,000 *less* at the end of twenty years compared to what they would have accumulated by simply investing in the S&P 500!

What's the story there? Why aren't the investors getting equity returns anywhere near the S&P 500?

It's easy to blame poor investment choices, which is a factor in some cases. But the primary factor that's proven to obliterate long-term returns is investor behavior. People's buy-sell decisions—getting in and out of good investments at the wrong times—are often the difference between achieving financial independence and struggling to ever be able to retire without sacrificing your lifestyle.

There are three primary reasons so many investors earn a poor return on behavior:

- Greed and fear cause people to make buying and selling mistakes.

- Misinformation in the form of market-timing strategies leads investors astray.

- Poor diversification creates excessive volatility for investors.

Why Managing Emotions Is Essential to Successful Long-Term Investing

According to the 21st Annual Quantitative Analysis of Investor Behavior (QUAIB) released by DALBAR, investors' behavioral mistakes tend to fall into one or more of nine categories. Some of these behaviors may be attributed to lack of experience or knowledge, but oftentimes they result from common psychological traits, traps, and triggers that affect all of us in one way or another.

These nine behaviors are summarized below in an excerpt from the report:

1. **Loss Aversion:** Expecting to find high returns with low risk

2. **Narrow Framing:** Making decisions without considering all implications

3. **Mental Accounting:** Taking undue risk in one area and avoiding rational risk in others

4. **Diversification:** Seeking to reduce risk, but simply using different sources

5. **Anchoring:** Relating to the familiar experiences, even when inappropriate

6. **Herding:** Copying the behavior of others, even in the face of unfavorable outcomes

7. **Regret:** Treating errors of commission more seriously than errors of omission

8. **Media Response:** Tendency to react to the news without reasonable examination

9. **Optimism:** Belief that good things happen to me and bad things happen to others[9]

While individual investors may experience differing combinations of these problems depending on their perspectives and personalities, the outcomes are in most cases the same: a fear of loss or the impulse to get in on the next big thing and therefore a rush into poor decisions, which leads to lower long-term returns and less financial independence.

The best example of this that I can think of is the Great Recession. (Unfortunately, there are millions of individual examples of these mistakes during that timeframe.) The years 2008 and 2009 presented the biggest buying opportunity in my thirty-year career. Some people took advantage of it by rebalancing their portfolios to include a healthy percentage of stocks, but most did not.

Most people followed the herd, reacted to the media's doom-and-gloom reports, and made decisions without considering the

---

9   See: http://www.dalbar.com/ProductsAndServices/QAIB.

longer-term effects: Historically, markets have always rebounded from crashes, and you can't benefit from the rebound unless you stay in the market.

Since 2009, I've met with hundreds of families and individuals who missed out—at least partially—on one of the greatest and longest bull markets in history. The chart below shows the damage even a short hiatus from the market did to portfolio performance in the following years.

Portfolio Value Comparison: Staying In vs. Getting Out for One Year

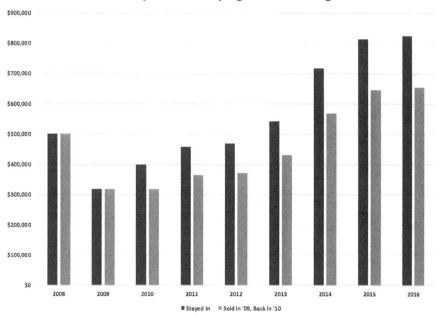

Note: The bars represent the portfolio value at the beginning of the year. The market lost value in 2008, so both portfolios took a hit to start 2009.

The chart represents the tale of two people who each had $500,000 in the stock market in the beginning of 2008. (I'm using the returns from the S&P 500 as a proxy for the purpose of simplicity.) The darker bar is the portfolio value of the investor who stayed in the market despite the crash, the media frenzy, and the herding pressures of seeing everyone else bail. The lighter bar is the portfolio of someone who generally trusts financial markets, but decided to get out in 2009 until the dust settled, then got back in to start 2010.

As the chart clearly shows, getting out for just one year—which seems like a reasonable idea given all of the fear at the time about the impending collapse of the entire economy—damaged the investor's portfolio forever. You can never turn back the clock and get those returns back.

For those who stayed out of the market for a longer period—and there are plenty of people who got spooked permanently—the chart looks even worse.

Overcoming Fear and Greed

We all have emotional reactions to the performance of our investments. I've been an investment advisor for more than thirty years, and I don't enjoy seeing my portfolio plummet 35% in a single year any more than the next person. But this is not about *eliminating* fear. It's about being able to step back, look at the big picture, and put your fears into perspective.

An investment advisor's role *should be* to calm clients' fears and to offer guidance and reassurance. If you're managing investments on your own, then the best way to do this is to adopt an objective, evidence-centered wealth management philosophy rather than work from a market outlook.

This means you're identifying a target mix of equities, fixed income, and cash in the spirit of providing yourself with the income and returns needed to achieve long- and short-term goals with the level of fluctuation you can stomach along the way.

When you have a philosophy in place and expect the unexpected to occur, it's easier to manage your natural emotional reactions and have perspective. My philosophy is called evidence-centered investing. Here are some evidentiary facts that I fall back on whenever clients get jittery about market volatility:

- Scientific studies prove that trying to time the stock market is a waste of time and money.[10]

- Nobody can predict when stocks have reached peak prices or valley lows, but we do know markets have always gone up in the long run.

- A diversified asset-allocation strategy can smooth out returns over time and capture a greater share of global market gains.

- With patience and objectivity, we can strategically wait for "the herd" to oversell or overbuy asset classes, then profit from the investment mistakes of others when prices become either too high (sell) or too low (buy) relative to the underlying value.

- There is no correlation between a fund manager's past performance and future results.[11]

- Passively managed index funds or ETFs usually outperform actively managed mutual funds.[12]

The remainder of this chapter is dedicated to discussing each of these points and how you can use them to your advantage.

10 Dimensional Fund Advisors, https://www.forbes.com/sites/feeonlyplanner/2015/11/02/access-the-3d
-dimension-in-investing-dimensional-fund-advisors/#540156585587.
11 Brian J. Knabe, Brent R. Brodeski, and Thomas A. Muldowney, "Evidence-Based Investing: A Scientific Framework for the Art of Investing" (Rockford, IL: Savant Capital Management, Inc., 2012).
12 Christopher B. Philips, Francis M. Kinniry Jr., Todd Schlanger, and Joshua M. Hirt, "The Case for Index-Fund Investing" (Malvern, PA: Vanguard, 2014).

Market Timing: Great in Theory, Bad in Practice

Sooner or later, you'll encounter the following advice on how to make money in the stock market: Move into the market while prices are low, and then sell your investments after they grow in value. Few will tell you it's easy, but many will try to sell you on this or that "system" so you can either invest for yourself and get rich or write them a check so they can do it for you.

Market timing is a great theory. The main trouble is that it doesn't work.

Numerous studies show that even guru market timers are frequently inaccurate—even the traders who've been on a roll for a few years and people who have their own TV or radio shows.

Ever been to a casino and witness a table "get hot"? Did it stay hot forever?

Even the brightest aren't good enough at market timing to make it work

In a study conducted by Nobel Laureate William Sharpe, he sought to find out how often a timing expert has to be right to break even relative to a benchmark portfolio.[13] The percentage he came up with is 74% of the time.

In an evaluation done on the top thirty-four market-timing gurus and their accuracy on forecasts ranging from 2000 to 2012, the highest grade anyone scored was just 68.2%. The average "guru" got it right less than half the time.[14]

Why is the market impossible to predict?

The stock market continuously sets prices based on the supply

---

13   Gary Lucido, "Does Market Timing Actually Work?" *Seeking Alpha*, January 9, 2008, http://seekingalpha.com/article/59493-does-market-timing-actually-work.
14   https://www.cxoadvisory.com/gurus.

and demand for stocks. In the short term, it's really not much different than the prices for baseball cards or any commodity that can be bought and sold. Supply is generally fixed in the short term, but the demand for each stock is fickle. The news, the momentum caused by the news, and the emotional reactions of millions of investors to these momentum shifts all factor into the rising or falling demand for stocks at any given moment.

In addition, there's also pure speculation. Market timers aren't speculating on stocks as much as they are speculating about other investors' speculations. It's not hard to see why no one has developed a scientific formula for predicting these movements.

There's no room for error; miss the days with the biggest gains, and it's hard to recover

According to a report by Oppenheimer, investors who missed out on the ten best days in the stock market between 1980 and 2010 saw their earnings fall to 5.7% from 8.2%.[15] On the flipside, missing the worst days will result in higher returns.

However, given how difficult it is to effectively time the market and since the overall market tends to rise over time, any attempt to do so may indeed backfire. Consider the previous example of two investors—including the one who decided to keep money on the sidelines in 2009 after the major crash of '08. That investor is still playing catch up.

---

15   Sam Ro, "If You Missed the Rally, Then You Probably Just Made the Most Classic Mistake in Investing," *Business Insider*, April 23, 2015, http://www.businessinsider.com/investors-always-miss-rallies-charts-2015-4.

Market timers rack up higher costs

Another disadvantage of market timing is the costs you'll assume. The more you trade, the more transaction fees you pay. Depending on how active you are, these fees could accumulate into a significant amount.

When you do make a profitable trade, you often end up paying more in taxes than you would on a long-term gain. In the US, long-term capital gains (from assets held for more than a year) are taxed at a much lower rate, while short-term capital gains (investments held for only a year or less) are taxed at the investor's ordinary income tax rate.

With market timing, you end up with a double whammy. Not only do you end up getting in and out of the market at the wrong times, you also end up having to spend more.

Stick with a Plan

The key to avoiding the mistakes covered in this chapter—and even profiting from the investment mistakes of others—is to develop a sound, long-term strategy that you're confident in. Devise a game plan for what you'll do when markets crash—as they inevitably do from time to time. Stick with that game plan through market turmoil, and avoid trendy investing.

How would you like to spend your retirement? Would you rather be doing what you enjoy or sitting in front of your computer trying to master the latest-and-greatest market-timing algorithm?

Devising a long-term strategy takes some time, thought, and research. Ideally, you develop your strategy with the help of an experienced financial planner to avoid making mistakes and to ensure your investing strategy aligns with your lifestyle goals. It should also be revisited from time to time, with flexibility built into it.

This takes some time and work upfront, but it ultimately affords you greater personal freedom to do more of what you love without financial worry.

A Closer Look at the Nine Behaviors That Hurt Investor Returns

Keep in mind, all of this is much easier said than done. We're all human; to be honest, being great investors is not something that is hardwired into our DNA. Investing isn't instinctual, but the behavioral mistakes we make are often the results of our natural instincts to avoid loss, experience pleasure, and seek strength in numbers.

So I think it's worth taking a closer look at nine investor behaviors and the negative impact those behaviors can have on returns. Everyone has been guilty of one or more of these behaviors at some point in time; but recognizing these tendencies is the first step toward overcoming them.

Loss aversion

There is a reason get-rich-quick schemes remain so popular, even in the face of overwhelming evidence. Our logical brain knows we should not expect high returns with minimal risk. Our emotional brain, on the other hand, is always looking for that quick fix, whether it's risking little to gain a lot or getting paid without doing work. Overcoming the desire for high risk-free returns is an essential part of investing success.

Narrow framing

We tend to see investments as entities on their own, without regard to the opportunity cost or alternative investments we could be making. When we stash money in a savings account, we feel confident that the money is safe. What we do not often consider is how much harder that money could be working or the impact that low interest rate will have on the performance of the overall portfolio. It's essential to consider all implications of an investment.

Mental accounting

Risk is relative. Sometimes we are incredibly risk averse in one area, but quite risky in another. Investors who make decisions entirely on their own are especially prone to this problem, as it's difficult to have a full view of the investment landscape when investing is something you do only in your free time from your "real job." Are you willing to invest the time it takes to learn about investing, or are you planning to do this in your spare time? If it is the latter, you may benefit from hiring a professional to manage your finances while you focus on your areas of true expertise.

Diversification

Diversification is a surprisingly difficult concept. Many people who think they are diversified turn out to be concentrating their risk in unexpected ways. Consider the investor who owns a basket of individual stocks, including drug companies, insurers, and biotech firms. He may think he is diversified, but a legislative change that impacts health insurance coverage is likely to have ripple effects across everything he owns. It would be far better for that investor to purchase stocks in a wide variety of industries, from consumer goods to real estate to technology and health care. Or even better, he should invest in exchange-traded funds (ETFs) that diversify for him.

Anchoring

Anchoring is a difficult trap to avoid, and even top economists and economic analysts are prone to this problem. We are psychologically predisposed to relate to, or anchor on, situations and events we already know and remember. The problem is that no two situations are the same, and no analogies are perfect. In other words, just because condition A led to result B last time does not mean the same will happen now. Avoiding anchoring and evaluating every investment decision on its own merits is essential to success.

Herding

There is a strong tendency to follow the crowd when making investment decisions, even when rational evidence suggests that the crowd is wrong and doing the opposite of what they are doing is the prudent course of behavior. We see this often in the investment sentiment numbers—the market often rallies when investor sentiment is at its most bearish.

Regret

We tend to regret the things we do much more than the things we do not do. In other words, we place a greater emphasis on errors of commission than on errors of omission. We regret buying that stock that turned out to be a bad investment, but we do not think about the opportunity we lost by not signing up for our 401(k) when we were first eligible. If you want to be a successful investor, you need to recognize opportunities wherever and whenever they occur and realize that the opportunity cost of doing nothing can be just as big as making an active mistake.

Media response

The news media is culpable for much of the current investment confusion. It is easy to take those talking heads and shouting matches much more seriously than they deserve. That is what the financial programs and cable news networks are counting on. In order to be successful as an investor, you need to seek out rational and balanced information, and that means looking beyond the doom and gloom and ignoring the "sky is falling" mentality so prevalent on TV and radio today.

Optimism

As a species, we tend toward optimism, and that is generally a good thing. Optimism helps us survive in the direst of circumstances and allows us to persevere even when it seems that all hope is lost. Unfortunately, that same optimism makes it difficult for us to imagine the worst-case scenarios that could derail our investments and wreck our retirement plans. It is even harder to imagine these scenarios if they are far into the future, or if they have never happened to us before. As an investor, you need to be optimistic about the long-term direction of the market, but it's even more important for you to be rational and realistic.

Overcoming Fear and Greed

As these nine common behaviors clearly show, managing our own emotions and expectations is just as important as managing our money. In fact, the two things are inextricably linked, and investor behavior is why the average investor vastly underperforms the actual market indexes.

It is our own behaviors, specifically our greed and fear, that cause us to miss out on the returns that are there for the taking. It is our fear of loss that causes us to flee for the exits when the market drops precipitously, and it is our greed that causes us to fall prey to get-rich-quick schemes and promises of high returns with no risk. It is our fear that makes us tune in to radio talk shows that claim financial Armageddon is just around the corner, or that hyperinflation is just over the horizon. And it is our greed that makes us believe the stock-picking gurus and talking heads on the financial cable stations, slavishly following their buy and sell recommendations, and then we wonder why our own returns fail to keep pace.

It is easy to see why these behaviors are so pervasive. Let's say you are chatting with a coworker about the choices in your 401(k). Your coworker tells you that she has just moved all of her stock market money to cash because she is worried about the upcoming presidential election. You, too, are worried about the results of that election, and you wonder if she might be onto something and if you should follow her lead.

Rationally, you might know that the results of presidential elections, even highly contested ones, have had little impact on investor returns. You have seen the studies that show that the party in power makes almost no difference to expected investment returns, and yet you still wonder. It is this tendency that smart investors constantly fight against, and they generally end up with better returns as a result of their vigilance.

None of these things are new, and fear and greed have been a part of our species since the beginning. Simply put, the nine behaviors outlined in this chapter are an integral part of our DNA, and overcoming them completely is simply not possible.

What we can do, however, is recognize those tendencies and stop them from wrecking our financial lives and retirement planning. We can recognize the tendency toward herding behavior when the next recession hits and investors are rushing to the exits. We can recognize our tendency toward loss aversion the next time someone tells us that we can earn a 10% return without any risk or the next time a friend touts a can't-miss investment opportunity. We can respond to our narrow framing tendency when all we want to do is hide out in cash and wait for the right investment. We can learn to see the opportunity cost involved in that decision and make a smarter and ultimately more effective decision instead.

In the end, one of the best ways to fight investor behavior and our tendency to be our own worst enemy is to hire a professional. Having a rational individual who can look at our finances and help us make sound and wise decisions is incredibly important in this media-saturated world, and it can prevent us from making some costly mistakes.

Hiring a Certified Financial Planner has real value, especially when it comes to advising against these harmful behaviors. Simply having someone you trust and can call the next time the market drops or a talk show host predicts the end of the world can be extremely valuable. There is not much you can do to change your DNA or banish harmful behaviors from your life, but hiring a professional to help you with your finances can prevent those behaviors from harming your future plans.

The Value of an Investment Policy Statement

One of the smartest things you can do to not only recognize but also actively avoid these investor behaviors is to develop a comprehensive Investment Policy Statement, particularly in collaboration with a trusted advisor. This statement should outline your investment goals and the methods you plan to use to achieve them. The Investment Policy Statement should also include clear guidelines for how and when you will make changes to your portfolio—because everyone else is doing it is not a good reason.

An Investment Policy Statement can be a valuable tool even during good times, but it is absolutely indispensable when the economy enters a soft patch and things start to look dire. Instead of running with the herd and heading for the exits, you can simply refer to your Investment Policy Statement and make wise adjustments to your portfolio—smart and carefully thought out changes that can boost your return and leave you in an even better financial position than you were before.

How You Behave as an Investor Isn't Everything

As a financial planner for the past thirty years, advising people on how to invest is a big part of what I do, but it's far from the totality. I've seen people with beautiful pie charts representing professional investment strategies outlive their money, despite being pretty good investors.

The next chapter goes into detail about additional financial planning strategies to help you make your nest egg last a lifetime and avoid outliving your assets.

How to Avoid Outliving Your Assets

"You can be young without money, but you can't be old without it."

—TENNESSEE WILLIAMS

IN THE PREVIOUS chapter, I discussed how to avoid major investing mistakes by introducing nine specific investor behaviors that can derail performance and cause us to underperform the market. I compared the returns of market indices and discussed how the vast majority of individual investors fall far short of capturing those gains to improve their lifestyles.

In this chapter, I'll get into personal financial planning strategies that will help you avoid what has become many retirees' greatest fear: outliving your assets.

This chapter will be broken down into the following sections:

- Determining your spending speed limit

- How much you can safely withdraw from your portfolio for income

- How aggressive your investment strategy should be

- Guaranteed income strategies and if/when to use them

- Sustaining your lifestyle despite market crashes

How to Determine Your Spending Speed Limit

While you're still working and retirement is far away, I always recommend paying yourself first: saving and investing 20% of your income and developing a personal lifestyle budget using the remaining 80%. So the spending speed limit for a thirty-five-year-old is easy to calculate: 80% of annual income. Most people don't save this much, but that's my recommendation if you want to one day feel completely comfortable with your financial independence and be able to continue your lifestyle on your own terms after you stop working. If you end up saving 15% instead, that's okay, but not as good. If you can save more than 20%, then you're really ahead of the game, as long as you're investing and making sure that money is working hard for you.

As we get older, especially as we approach and enter retirement, we have to be a lot more precise in determining our spending speed limit, because we're not just contributing to investment accounts but also withdrawing from them. Take too much too soon, and you could diminish your future income capability. Take too little, and you're shortchanging yourself.

Many people run out of money in retirement simply because they spend too much of their savings on a daily or monthly basis—not by buying sports cars and exotic vacations, but simply spending 7% of their portfolio each year instead of 5.5%, as a professional advisor may have recommended.

So, how much you can safely spend without depleting your portfolio and running out of money?

You have probably heard of the 4% rule—the guideline that suggests retirees start by withdrawing 4% of their portfolio in the first year of retirement, then increase that amount every five years or so to account for inflation. Under that scenario, a new retiree with a million-dollar portfolio would withdraw $40,000 the first year of retirement and ramp up the amount to cover inflation in subsequent years.

The 4% withdrawal rule is a good place to start, but it is only a basic guideline. The amount an individual can safely withdraw from a given portfolio will vary according to a number of factors including:

- Asset allocation

- Age and life expectancy

- Desire to leave an inheritance

- Other income streams

- Any unique circumstances

How asset allocation affects your speed limit

An investment portfolio composed of low-yielding government bonds, for example, may be far less robust than one that is composed of a fifty-fifty mix of stocks and bonds. The 4% rule assumes a 6% rate of return on your portfolio, spending 4% and reinvesting 2% to keep up with inflation in future years. So if your portfolio is designed to earn less than 6%, then the 4% rule may not be appropriate.

Your age and your speed limit

If you plan to start withdrawing from your portfolio at a tender young age, your speed limit may be less than 4%. This is because the younger you are, the more years you'll need to be tapping into your portfolio as an income stream. This means you'll live through more inflation, more recessions, more stock crashes, and have a higher likelihood of facing some type of financial emergency during your withdrawal years.

How leaving an inheritance affects your speed limit

This one is totally subjective and largely depends on your values and circumstances. You may have a special-needs child or grand-child who will need the money after you pass away, or you may have received an inheritance yourself and want to pass the favor down the line. Conversely, you may simply believe in self-reliance or be lucky enough to have kids who are successful enough to not need an inheritance. In the latter situation, you can spend more of your portfolio each year because you're not looking to preserve capital for the next generation.

What are your other income streams?

If you're lucky enough to have a lifelong pension that, combined with Social Security, pays for your family's lifestyle, then your portfolio may simply be an added bonus for you, or even an emergency fund. Most people these days do not have lifelong guaranteed pensions, but if you do, then your speed limit may be more aggressive. Can you continue living your lifestyle without tapping into your portfolio at all?

Does the value of your home affect your speed limit?

Your home is likely a significant percentage of your overall net worth, and you may be able to leverage its value to increase your income capability in retirement and avoid outliving your assets in the following ways:

- Renting a portion of your home for income

- Selling your home and downsizing to something less expensive

- Converting the equity in your home into an income stream[16]

How much guaranteed income do you need?

As mentioned previously, guaranteed income is a huge asset when striving for financial independence. At this point, I've discussed return on behavior at great lengths, and how sticking to your long-term financial plan is easier said than done.

---

16 Regarding the third bullet, it's essential to understand the risks and legal ramifications of converting your home into an income stream. Be sure to speak with an advisor you trust who has no conflict of interest before entering into this type of contract.

Of the many statistics I can share about how the market has always risen over time, nothing calms nerves quite like guaranteed income. If you can rely on a check hitting your mailbox every month that will pay your bills for you, you'll be more comfortable in every aspect of your financial life. And you'll be more likely to stomach the investing risks needed to keep pace with rising prices and taxes with your other income-producing assets.

What are your potential sources of guaranteed income?

You can start by determining exactly how much you can expect in Social Security benefits when you become eligible at SSA.gov. From there, you can access a detailed benefits estimate that is based on your actual earnings, giving you a pretty good idea of what you can expect to collect when you become eligible.

Remember, delaying your Social Security benefits is usually a smart move financially. Your guaranteed benefit goes up each year you delay, topping out at age seventy. If you wait until age seventy to begin collecting benefits, you will get monthly checks that are 32% higher than if you had started collecting at age sixty-two. The break-even age for those who delay collecting the full eight years is around age seventy-seven, meaning even though you started getting checks eight years later than the earliest day possible, by age seventy-seven, the sum of the higher monthly payments equals what you left on the table for those eight years. After age seventy-seven, the higher monthly payments are all "profit," and your cost-of-living adjustments each year become exponentially larger, because the percentage increases are being made on a higher dollar amount.

As mentioned earlier, and I can't say this enough, it's well worth it to sit down with a Social Security expert or a Certified Financial Planner to discuss the ins and outs of this valuable retirement asset. You really only have one chance to make the right decision for yourself and your family. With potential gains of six figures and beyond at stake, make sure you understand all of your options and the consequences and benefits of each.

Keep in mind, this is not only about getting more money from the government over a lifetime; it's also about having a higher guaranteed income stream and putting less stress on your portfolio to fund your lifestyle later in life. So the planners in my office and I, as we're helping clients plan to never run out of money, almost always recommend delaying Social Security as long as possible for these reasons.

After you have a good idea how much you can expect from Social Security, you can move on to any company pensions for which you are eligible. If you are eligible for a traditional pension, you will want to factor that into the equation and include it in your guaranteed income calculations. You will want to determine whether your pension benefit is indexed to inflation and whether or not your spouse will continue to receive a portion of the benefit in the event of your death.

Do you need more guaranteed income than you're currently positioned to receive?

Now add up your Social Security and pensions and put that into your guaranteed income bucket. Then, compare that amount to the amount you expect to spend each year in retirement.

On an annual basis, what percentage of your portfolio is this shortfall?

Can you stomach the market volatility required to achieve the type of return needed to withdraw this amount from your portfolio each year?

Use the chart that follows as a guide to answer this question.

WITHDRAWAL RATE	PORTFOLIO STRATEGY NEEDED
>2%	**Conservative or Ultra-Conservative.** This means less than half of your portfolio will be exposed to the stock market's volatility, with the majority of your wealth being in fixed-income and other low-risk investments. This limits your upside and may make it difficult to keep pace with inflation, especially when interest rates are low; but it protects you from massive losses in down years for the stock market.
3%–4%	**Moderately Conservative.** With about half of your portfolio invested for long-term growth in the stock market and half in fixed-income/low-risk funds, this type of portfolio is ideal for the standard practice of spending no more than 4% annual withdrawals and rebalancing naturally by selling bonds for income during down years in the market and selling equities for income during good times. You'll experience bigger losses during down years and higher gains during good years than if you were in a conservative portfolio.
5%–6%	**Moderately Aggressive or Aggressive.** If you're spending 6% of your portfolio each year, you'll likely need an aggressive investing strategy. This means investing mostly in stocks, expecting higher average annual returns, but seeing your portfolio suffer major hits during crashes. This requires a lot of faith in the market and nerves of steel when you don't have a steady paycheck coming in to support your lifestyle.

Note that if you only need to withdraw a small amount, such as 2%, you don't have to be in a conservative portfolio. You can choose a higher risk-higher reward portfolio if you're comfortable with that level of risk, and the additional gains from your riskier investments will likely make you wealthier, increase your income capability with time, or allow you to leave a larger inheritance. The chart is meant to outline the minimum risk required to achieve the types of returns you need.

What if your speed limit is too slow to live the lifestyle you want?

As a goals-based financial planner, I never like to break the news to a client or a prospect that what they've worked so hard to achieve is beyond reach. Unfortunately, that is sometimes the case. However, the earlier you start planning and running analyses like this, the better chance you have to adapt your strategies to unpleasant realities, change course, and achieve your dreams.

If the speed limit on your withdrawal rate cannot fill the gap between your guaranteed income and your lifestyle needs, or if you are uncomfortable with the level of risk you need to assume in order to raise your speed limit to the appropriate level, here are a few options to consider:

- Find ways to cut back your spending so that you need less income from withdrawals.

- Work longer to build up your nest egg and increase your income capability.

- Phase into retirement by working part-time so that you can delay or reduce withdrawals.

Generating Income That Keeps Up with Rising Prices

Many investors, especially those in retirement, are so fearful of risk that they move too much of their money into perceived "safe" investments—things like bank certificates of deposit, low-yielding government bonds, and money market funds. Those are all safe investments in that there is no risk of principal loss; but when you take the long road, it is easy to see that their safety is often an illusion.

Take the example of Ted, a chemical engineer who always earned a good living and consistently lived below his means. Ted invested in a few stocks over the years, mostly individual efforts he thought were undervalued and primed for a big move. More often than not, however, Ted got it wrong, and he now takes a dim view of stock market investments and the risk he sees there.

As a result, Ted has almost all of his money in government bonds and bank CDs, investments that are guaranteed to get him his money back plus a little bit of interest. Ted thinks he is doing well, but in reality he is losing purchasing power every year and falling further behind.

Let's assume that Ted's portfolio of bank CDs and government bonds is currently yielding 1.5%, a generous assumption in this world of near-zero interest rates. Even given that rosy scenario, a 3% annual rate of inflation means Ted is falling 1.5% behind each year in terms of purchasing power, a figure that can really add up over time, especially when you factor in the potential for tax increases from local, state, and federal governments.

As you can see, Ted is scared of market volatility, and that fear has caused him to lose purchasing power. If Ted can manage his emotions and fear of markets, he can actually let market volatility work to his advantage. It would have been far better for Ted to accept some market risk in return for a higher potential return.

Here's what Ted should be doing instead: I call it the bucket strategy. It's also relatively the same as asset allocation, but the word *bucket* provides some good imagery to go along with the concept. For the income Ted needs to live on in the short term, such as living expenses and recreational fun this year, he makes sure to have enough money in lower-risk investments such as bonds or even cash. This way, he can still live his lifestyle even if markets crash. He won't be forced to sell stocks at a loss to fund his lifestyle; he's avoiding selling low. For long-term goals and lifestyle expenses five, ten, or twenty years down the road, Ted should probably accept more risk so that his assets can grow and outpace inflation.

In an extreme case like Ted's, he may consider purchasing some certainty and shedding some risk with some combination of annuities or insurance.

I mentioned earlier in this book that although annuities are expensive, they do have a place in some portfolios. I hope this chapter has shed some light on what I meant by that. There are some "advisors" out there who make their living trying to sell you the biggest annuities possible; if you have $100,000, they'll try to sell you an annuity worth $100,000; if you have $750,000, they'll try to sell you an annuity worth $750,000. My philosophy on annuities is to buy only as much as you need for peace of mind, while retaining enough flexibility in your finances so that you can still make adjustments along the way.

So let's say Ted will get $2,000 per month in Social Security benefits, but needs $2,500 a month for basic expenses. In this case, he should receive just enough guaranteed income in the form of annuities to plug the gap between Social Security and basic needs. This way, Ted knows that no matter how poorly the market performs, he will always be able to pay the bills. In this instance, the right level of guaranteed income may increase his willingness to take the risks necessary to keep up with rising prices.

Additional risk factors that could derail your retirement

While it is impossible to predict everything that could happen during your three or four decades of retirement, there are some common risks that every would-be retiree needs to prepare for. The major risks your retirement portfolio is likely to face include the following:

- Longevity risk

- Sequence of return risk

- The risk of high taxes

- The risk of market volatility

Longevity risk or longevity reality

Let's start with longevity risk. In some cases this is a happy risk—it means you live longer than you anticipated. It also makes it harder to avoid running out of money—sorry to be such a pessimist!

To be honest, life expectancies have risen to the point where I no longer even consider this a risk. I call it *longevity reality*. And the longer you live, the more exposure you have to all other risks discussed in this chapter: The longer you live, the more you save in taxes by implementing tax minimization strategies, the more market crashes you may live through, the higher prices will get, and the longer the compounding effect of negative return on behavior will have on your portfolio.

So it's critical to plan for a long life and many years of inflation (my apologies if that sounds really cynical) by reinvesting one-third of your investment gains, Social Security check, or pension payments back into an investment account. This will help you keep up with rising prices and taxes.

Sequence-of-returns risk

Sequence-of-returns risk refers to the risk of getting lower or even negative returns when you first start to withdraw money from an account. A bad first few years in retirement is more damaging than a bad few years a decade in. This is because the returns generated from your portfolio during the good years is a percentage of the value of the portfolio; if your portfolio loses value in those first few years, its ability to generate predictable income declines.

Let's take a look at Albert and Nancy, a hypothetical couple who entered retirement just as the market was tanking. They had $2 million in their combined retirement funds, and they thought they were well prepared for the end of their working lives. Their advisor had told them they could safely spend $100,000 per year from their portfolio after assessing their risk tolerance and legacy goals.

But as the economy entered a deep recession and the stock portion of their portfolios started tanking, they suddenly found themselves in an uncomfortable position: With only $1,200,000 left in their portfolio at the bottom of the decline, spending $100,000 in their first year of retirement as they had planned (i.e., their spending speed limit) would be 8.3% of their portfolio, potentially reducing their nest egg to $1,100,000 at the end of the year if the market didn't rebound quickly.

At $1,100,000, their new speed limit, should they remain consistent with a 5% withdrawal rate, would be only $55,000, a 45% drop in lifestyle spending.

Should they go ahead with their plan to spend $100,000 and put additional stress on their portfolio in future years, or should they stay consistent with a 5% withdrawal rate and accept a lesser lifestyle?

The best strategy to avoid this type of tough decision early in retirement is to implement a bucket strategy. This means you're determining where to put your assets based on when you need the income those assets will generate for you. That means the money you need for this year's, and even next year's, income should not be exposed to volatile stock market risks. When you're not relying on the market to produce income for the next two years of life-style expenses, then a crash does not necessarily affect your spending speed limit. You withdraw from your low-risk investments or cash balances that are generating lower but steady returns. This allows your stocks time to recover lost value.

How many years of income should you have in lower-risk invest-ments to avoid selling your stocks low?

Consider the recovery time of some memorable crashes:

- Black Monday 1987 (fifteen months)

- Great Recession (two years)

- 1970s recession (three years)

- Dotcom bubble (five years)

- Great Depression (seven years)[17]

This doesn't mean you must hedge against the next Great Depres-sion, because the risk of a market crash must be balanced against all other risks, such as inflationary pressures and longevity risk. All things considered, if you eliminate all risk, you're probably playing it too safe. But I hope these statistics shed light on the fact that your retire-ment will likely last two to six times longer than the recovery time of

17   Matt Egan, "Worried about a Stock Market Crash? Read This," *CNN Money*, February 26, 2015, http://money.cnn.com/2015/02/26/investing/stock-market-crash-bubble-investing.

even the Great Depression. And in all likelihood, the bear markets you encounter will be much shorter than that one (hopefully).

Making market volatility your friend by profiting from the mistakes of other investors

The bucket strategy can help mitigate the effects of a downturn, but we can also take it a step further and actually profit from volatility by capitalizing on the investment mistakes of others. It sounds brutal, I know. But capitalism is a brutal, unforgiving system. It's still the best option we know of, but brutal nonetheless.

How do we capitalize on the investment mistakes of others?

First, you have to do everything right: have the right asset allocation strategy, avoid emotional decisions, and pass on the market timing strategies. As mentioned in the previous chapter on return on behavior, when stocks fall for any reason, some investors will sell out of fear of further losses, which leads to more fear and more selling. The "death spiral" will vary in its duration and impact, but what happens is that people sell irrationally, not due to market fundamentals or the underlying value of the assets being sold. Assets become "on sale" and are undervalued.

When this happens, your portfolio will become out of balance in terms of your asset allocation. If your asset allocation strategy was sixty-forty, as stocks lose value, it may go to fifty-fifty, for example. Once a year, you should rebalance your portfolio. By doing this, you end up buying undervalued stocks poised for a rebound at some point in the future. The rebound may not happen right away, but fundamentals drive the long-term direction of equities.

The opposite is true during bull markets, when fear causes less disciplined investors to drive up prices beyond their underlying value. Your asset allocation may end up being seventy-thirty, and when you rebalance to sixty-forty, you'll be selling high. So this natural process of rebalancing and sticking with your asset allocation strategy causes you to buy low and sell high in a disciplined way. The mistakes of other investors present you with opportunities.

How Should You Invest?

I've discussed the heart of my financial planning philosophies on avoiding mistakes and mitigating risks. Now it's time to get more granular and get into where to turn for advice or how to construct your own portfolio.

I'll start with the former in the next chapter, which covers the myth of the great money manager—the common belief that a small group of financial wizards have it all figured out, and that the key to your success as an investor is to learn how to pick stocks like them, invest in the funds they manage, or listen to their advice when they speak.

I will dispel this myth once and for all and reveal more practical advice that I'm hoping will allow you to make fewer behavioral mistakes and know where to turn for better advice that positions you to achieve your lifestyle goals.

The Myth of the Great Money Manager

"The broker said the stock was 'poised to move.'

Silly me, I thought he meant up."

–RANDY THURMAN

THERE IS A pervasive myth in the world of investing, and it is costing investors billions of dollars in the form of higher costs, lower returns, and wasted efforts. That myth is that if an investor could just find the perfect money manager, the perfect mutual fund, or the perfect stock, then all their problems would be solved and they would be able to live happily ever after.

The truth is that there is no such thing as the perfect money manager, and the mutual fund that enjoyed gangbuster returns last year is unlikely to experience a repeat performance next year or the year after that. If you want to invest for the long run and enjoy the returns that are there for the taking, you need to get your emotions under control, stop searching for the perfect investment, and take a more practical approach instead.

Why It Doesn't Pay to Hunt for Great Money Managers

When you invest in a mutual fund, the fund manager invests your money in a diversified portfolio of stocks, bonds, and/or alternative investments that are designed to outperform market averages. Historic evidence shows that fund managers usually fail at achieving this goal—especially over the long haul and when you factor in the expense fees of these funds.

Index Funds Trump the Efforts of Professional Money Managers

According to "The Case for Index Fund Portfolios," a white paper by Portfolio Solutions, less expensive, passively managed index funds—the benchmarks money managers are paid to beat—outperform actively managed funds almost all the time.[18]

In studying advanced portfolios holding ten asset classes in a span of twenty-five years, researchers found—

- The probability of the most basic index fund portfolio outperforming an actively managed portfolio began at the eightieth percentile. This probability grew as additional asset classes were added to the portfolio.

---

18   "The Right Kind of Portfolio Diversification," *Betterment*, June 21, 2013, https://www.betterment.com /resources/investment-strategy/all-index-fund-lineup-best-for-portfolio-health-white-paper.

- The probability of an all-index fund portfolio beating an all-mutual fund portfolio increases with the length of time the portfolios compete against one another. This probability grew as the time period studied lengthened from five years to fifteen years.

This means that the longer you hold your index fund investments, the better your shot is at outperforming active funds.

Both of these points solidify the argument for index funds: The larger the sample size (either by adding more funds to a portfolio, or studying for an increased length of time), the more likely index funds are to outperform managed mutual funds.

When a managed mutual fund does outperform the corresponding index, it's likely due to chance, or a temporary alignment between the fund manager's philosophy and market conditions, rather than the type of skill that will stand the test of time.

What about the cream of the crop of money managers?

In most industries, track records usually give you an idea of what to expect from an individual, but this unfortunately does not apply to money managers. As a result, many investors waste long hours searching for the next Warren Buffett.

It's true that some managers beat benchmarks some of the time—or even for many years in a row—but this does not translate to financial genius. Too often investors, and the media, mistake luck for acumen.

Money managers who outperform their peers and the index usually regress to the mean. As a matter of fact, regularly updated research shows that great money managers' levels of persistence in beating the index is lower than what is expected from mere chance.

It is easy to see why the myth of the great money manager has persisted even in the face of evidence to the contrary. After all, the financial press and money-oriented TV channels are always highlighting the latest superstar or stock-picking guru. There is nothing exciting about an index fund, and you are unlikely to see an interview with an index fund manager any time soon (for the simple reason that these funds do not have high-priced managers).

When you delve into the evidence, however, you will quickly see why the simple approach is often the best one. That evidence clearly shows that at some point during the course of their careers, nearly every top-performing money manager underperformed their peers for years at a time. If you try to buy past performance, you will be sorely disappointed.

According to the findings reported in "The Case for Index Fund Portfolios," even the best and most successful money managers are not able to sustain their performance advantages over the long term. Specifically, the findings show that while some money managers do manage to outperform their benchmarks on occasion, that outperformance is rarely exceptional, and it rarely lasts for very long.

A top money manager may, for instance, achieve an annual total return of 15% in a year when the market was up 12% or 13% as a whole. They may continue that outperformance for the next couple of years, but in the end they are likely to revert to the mean and underperform their peers in the future. That reversion to the mean erases the previous benefits of holding an actively managed fund and reinforces the value of an index fund approach to stock market investing.

In the end, the difficulties involved in identifying the top money managers make clear that this type of investment approach is unlikely to be productive over the long run. In any given year, there are bound to be money managers who outperform their peers and beat their benchmarks, sometimes by a wide margin. In retrospect, it is easy to see those top-performing managers as superstars, but when we take the long view, their performance suddenly seems a bit less amazing. A few years of superior performance followed by years of underperformance means that those former high fliers are unlikely to do better than low-cost index funds in the end.

How are some money managers able to outperform their peers?

Consider this: If all 4,000+ money managers were asked to flip a coin ten consecutive times, wouldn't it be likely that a few of them would get ten heads in a row (or ten tails in a row)? Should we exalt these money managers as expert coin flippers and feature them on the covers of prestigious magazines? Of course not, but that's exactly what the media does with flash-in-the-pan mutual fund rock stars who've hit a lucky streak.

Do the gurus really have it right?

Reading the financial press and watching investing shows on TV can be entertaining, but should you take these sources seriously? In the end, are these financial programs truly providing investment advice, or is what they are dishing out mere entertainment? A look at the facts behind the hype can be instructive here.

Chances are you have encountered putative investment gurus screaming "Buy!" at the top of their lungs over on the corner of the screen. The show host may be an investment-programming superstar, but is his advice really all that it is made out to be?

The short answer is no. A recent analysis reported by Market-Watch found that viewers may want to think twice before following their favorite pundits. That MarketWatch analysis looked at forty-nine separate stocks that one particularly—*ahem*—outspoken pundit had previously identified as top prospects. These were touted as stocks to buy right now, and many investors no doubt took the advice and made bets with their own money.

We can only hope that those investors were gambling with money they could afford to lose, because lose they did. Retired finance professor David O. England decided to put this forty-nine stock list to the test, investing a hypothetical $1,000 in each one of those supposed top picks. England even upped the ante by attempting to place a bet with this TV host. If the TV host's stock picks turned out to be profitable, England would pick up the tab for dinner.

The supposed stock-picking guru never responded to the bet, and in the end that turned out to be a good thing (for him). Only four-teen of the forty-nine stock picks had a higher price six months after the initial recommendation. That equates to a dismal 28% rate of success, or far less than mere chance would suggest.

While the results of that six-month stock-trading test are truly appalling, the news would be even worse for a true active investor. While the losses Mr. England experienced were of the paper variety, the losses of a real stock trader would be very real. And the news gets even worse. The test of the stock picks included only the purchase price of the shares themselves, not the commissions involved on both sides of the trade. Had this been a real-world test, the costs would have been far higher and the performance would have been that much worse.

The purpose of this story is not to disparage any particular show host or his stock-picking prowess. I'm sure this media personality had some successes along the way, and he continues to point to them as proof of his abilities. Rather, the purpose is to show the folly of investing in individual stocks based on insider tips, TV or radio commentators, or a host of other criteria. Making a bet on a stock once in a while may be good fun, but doing so with money you cannot afford to lose is a monumentally bad idea.

Passively managed, low-cost index funds aren't very exciting, but at the end of the day, it's all about results. The simple way of doing things is often the best, and the evidence tells us this is also true for picking stocks.

Why Do So Many Prominent Investors and Institutions Still Push Mutual Funds?

There are a few reasons. First, there's ego. Most prominent fund managers are extremely intelligent. They went to top colleges, graduated at the tops of their classes, and earned advanced degrees.

A portion of these money managers genuinely believe they are smart enough to beat the market over time—clever enough to buy low and sell high consistently throughout their professional careers. They've read the same studies I've read and think *they* are the exceptions who've figured out the secrets to outperforming the market.

Over time, these "great" money managers very often get served a big slice of humble pie.

Second, the powers that be have too much skin in the game to come forward and admit that index funds and passively managed exchange-traded funds (ETF) are the right choice for most investors. Mutual funds manage $31 trillion in assets.[19] If fund companies embraced the evidence and research that shows they're not very good at beating the benchmarks they get paid to beat, where would that leave them?

Mutual funds and hidden fees

Whether you are investing for retirement, the education of your children, or any other long-term goal, chances are mutual funds represent the heart of your portfolio. Mutual funds are the core of most 401(k) and 403(b) plans, and they are routinely used for IRA accounts and personal investing as well.

Mutual funds can have a lot of benefits for the individual investor, but they also have their fair share of problems, including the hidden fees that most investors are not even aware of. These hidden fees can drive up the cost of mutual fund investing, making them more expensive than ETFs and other investment options.

If you invest in mutual funds, you need to be aware of the potential for hidden fees. Examining the prospectus for your mutual funds may not be scintillating, but it is important, and that is a good place to start.

Once you delve into the details, you will probably find that your mutual funds have a number of hidden expenses, over and above the expense ratio stated in the prospectus and other documents. These hidden fees include: the cost of trading as they buy and sell stocks, bonds, and other investments; load fees incurred when investors buy the fund; exit fees when they sell; and the taxes paid on short-term capital gains when the mutual fund manager makes changes in an effort to improve performance.

---

19 Investment Company Institute, "Worldwide Mutual Fund Assets and Flows Second Quarter 2014," October 2014, https://www.statista.com/statistics/235553/assets-managed-in-mutual-funds-worldwide.

In addition to these hidden fees, there is the undeniable fact that actively managed funds are almost always more expensive to own than their index fund counterparts. While index funds can cost as little as .10% a year to own, it is not unusual for an actively managed mutual fund to charge ten or even twenty times that amount.

Even a small increase in costs can have a huge impact on your portfolio over time, yet many investors underestimate just how much mutual fund fees are costing them. If the actively traded mutual fund you own charges thirty-five basis points (.35%) more per year than its ETF or index fund equivalent, that means an added cost of $3.50 for every $1,000 invested. That may not seem like much, but on a portfolio of $100,000, that is an extra $350 a year; over the course of thirty years, this equates to more than $10,000 less in your investments.

The news is even worse when you consider the opportunity cost of that wasted money. If you had invested that extra $350 a year in a diversified portfolio, chances are you would have far more than $10,000 over the course of three decades. The evidence is clear—investors ignore mutual fund fees at their peril.

Should You Pick Individual Stocks Yourself?

Do you ever wish you had been the first person to invest in Amazon.com? Or the smart person who bought Apple stock when it was in the toilet? Or a personal friend of Mark Zuckerberg, with access to a couple thousand shares of the IPO? If so, you are not alone. Everyone dreams of getting in on the ground floor of the next big thing, and a few lucky individuals manage to make it happen, turning a small investment into a hugely valuable holding.

The bad news is that those kinds of events are all too rare. While

Amazon.com turned out to be a huge success, Pets.com went out of business, and its most valuable asset turned out to be that annoying sock puppet. For every winning stock pick, there are dozens of losers, and that can make trying to choose your own stocks an exercise in frustration and financial loss.

There are a number of reasons why picking individual stocks and making a consistent profit is such a hard thing to do. For starters, there are the commissions that must be paid every time a block of shares changes hands. The Internet has lowered these commission costs substantially, but they can still add up for active traders. These are all costs that must be overcome before you can break even on the trade.

Even if you manage to get your trading costs down to a very low level, there are a number of other obstacles to overcome. When you trade a stock, you need to be right not just once but twice. You need to be right about the best time to buy the stock, but just as importantly you need to be right about when to sell and book your profits.

If you are a stock trader, you have probably experienced this frustration for yourself. You keep your eyes on a hot prospect, looking for the perfect time to buy. You watch and watch as the stock rises ever higher, then finally pull the trigger and make your purchase. Suddenly, as if on cue, the stock drops precipitously, leaving you feeling like the clothes shopper who paid full price for a suit the day before the big sale.

The opposite happens just as often. You have a hefty profit in a stock that turned out to be a winner. You want to book your profit, so you sell your shares, only to see them rocket higher the very next day. Or you finally give up on that dog you bought last year, only to see the price skyrocket the day after you sell it.

It can all get frustrating pretty quickly, and we have not even gotten to taxes yet. Every time you sell a stock in a non-retirement account, you get the attention of the taxman, and he is bound to want his cut. Taxes on capital gains may be lower than those on traditional income, but that is cold comfort when you are writing that big check to the IRS.

You can argue about the fairness of taxes on capital gains all you want, but that does not mean they are going away. If you trade individual stocks, you need to take taxes into account, and that can make the entire enterprise far less attractive.

Even if the stock you chose turns out to be a huge winner, when you sell, you will likely incur a huge tax bill for your troubles. You may still have a hefty profit to show for your hard work and risk taking, but the amount you make may be depressingly small after the tax bill has been paid.

Keep in mind as well that individual stocks can, and do, go to zero—something that even the most poorly managed mutual fund or ETF is extremely unlikely to do. If you invest in an individual stock, you must accept the risk that you can lose all the money you put in. Hopefully, that will not happen, but it is always a possibility. That is why it is so important to carefully evaluate your entire investment portfolio, including your retirement fund holdings, mutual funds, annuities, and everything else. If you do decide to invest in individual stocks on your own, keeping each holding to 4–5% of your overall portfolio is a smart way to mitigate your risks and avoid a serious loss should something go wrong.

As you can see, the costs associated with buying and selling individual stocks can be high, the risks outsized compared to mutual funds and ETFs, and the profits often less than you might think. That is not to say that no one should buy and sell individual stocks. Many people do so quite successfully. What it does mean, however, is that your stock-picking activities should be limited to a small part of your portfolio.

If you love the excitement of picking individual stocks and you are fairly good at it, then make sure to differentiate between your "real money" and your "play money." Use a separate account to buy and sell individual stocks without putting your family's lifestyle or your larger portfolio at risk. The key is never investing in individual stocks with money you cannot afford to lose.

If you get lucky and find the next Amazon.com, Facebook, Apple, or Microsoft, you can cash out your millions and enjoy a life of leisure. If you choose the next Pets.com or Boo.com, you can lick your wounds, enjoy a nice glass of wine, and know that your larger portfolio will be no worse for wear. And you can continue living the lifestyle you enjoy today without sacrificing your most precious goals.

Maintaining a diversified investment portfolio is vitally important, as is rebalancing that portfolio to keep the percentages you have identified in large-cap stocks, small-cap stocks, mid-cap stocks, government bonds, corporate bonds, and other asset classes. If you have a high risk tolerance and some money to play with, you might want to include individual stocks in your investment portfolio as well. If you do, it is important to be aware of the risks involved and to keep the amount you put in to a minimum. Buying and selling individual stocks can be a lot of fun and very exciting, but it should not put your chosen lifestyle, or your net worth, at risk.

Opportunity to Capture

MINIMIZE YOUR INCOME TAXES

"You don't *pay* taxes. They *take* taxes."

—CHRIS ROCK

I'LL SAY IT again: It's not how much you earn, it's how much you keep that counts. It does not matter how much money you earn as income or how much value your investment gained before taxes; earning a dollar to get taxed 40% is less desirable than earning $0.75 and getting taxed 10%. The money you send to Uncle Sam can't pay for your vacation or your daughter's wedding, nor can it produce income for you.

Minimizing your taxes should be an integral part of any financial planning strategy. If you have not considered the tax implications of what you are doing, your investment strategy is incomplete. You

obviously have to pay taxes, but—for yourself and for your family—
don't pay more than you owe.

A Vital Part of Your Financial Plan

Taxes are such an important part of successful financial planning
that they represent 10% of the Lifestyle Sustainability Scorecard.
By putting your money in the right types of accounts and implementing an intelligent withdrawal strategy, you can reduce your tax
liability while spending the same amount of money on your lifestyle.

Whether you are in your peak earning years and just starting to
save for the future, in your preretirement years and trying to make
the most of your investments, or already enjoying your golden years,
incorporating tax-saving strategies into your financial plan can save
you a lot of money. Every dollar you save on taxes is one more dollar
you will have to save, invest, and ultimately enjoy.

If you have been following politics for any length of time, you
have probably noticed that the politicians in Washington, DC seem
to think they can spend our money more wisely than we can, but
the majority of investors do not agree. If you want to make the most
of your investment income, you need to put yourself, not the president, Congress, or any other politician, first.

Evading taxes is illegal, but tax avoidance is both legal and ethi-
cal. Think of it this way: There is no one on earth who is more com-
mitted to the financial welfare of your family than you are, and you
owe it to your loved ones to maximize your income and look out for
their future success.

Also consider that taxes are the single largest expense for many
families. Most of us immediately think of federal and state income

taxes that we pay with each paycheck, but remember that it's more than just that: Dividends get taxed, we pay taxes on capital gains and state sales taxes, and of course there are local property taxes. These can all be huge bills that we pay. The fewer taxes you pay, the more money you have to spend on things like the education of your children, the establishment of savings accounts for your grandchildren, and your and your spouse's retirement.

Saving Now and Later

Retirees generally have more flexibility when it comes to tax bracket management, but you do not have to wait until retirement to start saving on taxes and reducing your taxable income. There are things you can do right now to reduce your current tax bill and maximize the value of your current investments and your future returns. And there are ways to position your finances as you approach retirement so that you'll have maximum flexibility for retirement tax strategies when that time comes.

One of the beautiful things about reducing your current taxes is that the savings grow and compound over time. That extra dollar you save on your taxes today is more than a dollar. In the future, that dollar will be worth far more due to the returns from your investment of that dollar, and the sooner you start your tax-saving strategy the better the results will be.

No Substitute for Professional Help and Guidance

You should of course keep in mind that while the information contained in this chapter, and this entire book, is intended to help you save money on your taxes, there is no substitute for professional one-on-one tax advice from recognized experts in the field. Feel free to use this information as a guide, but always follow up with a Certified Financial Planner, CPA, estate planning attorney, or other expert.

As a matter of fact, it is a good idea to consult with each of these experts, and the best approach is to have them work for you as a team. Having these experts coordinate with you, and with one another, is the best way to develop a comprehensive tax-minimization and financial planning strategy that fits your needs, your expectations, and your desired pre- and postretirement lifestyle.

No matter what stage of life you are in, the opportunities to reduce your taxable income and minimize your tax bill are almost endless. Once you start looking for these tax-saving opportunities, you will wonder how you missed out on them for so long.

Tax Savings Opportunities in Retirement

While it is possible to minimize your taxes no matter what stage of life you are in, there is no doubt that tax minimization will be easier in your retirement years. Let's take a look at John and Sarah, a recently retired couple who have always worked hard, made a lot of money, and paid a very high rate of taxes. When John and Sarah were working, they had limited ways to lower their tax bill. They wrote off their mortgage interest, took credit for their charitable contributions, and contributed to health savings accounts, but they still ended up with a hefty tax bill year after year.

Now that John and Sarah are retired, they can use strategic withdrawals from retirement and non-retirement accounts to lower their tax rates and keep more of the money they worked so hard to earn all those years. Examples of retirement accounts are Traditional IRA or a 401(k) accounts where you can contribute tax-free up to a certain annual limit, and see your investments grow tax-free until it's time to withdraw.

John and Sarah need to withdraw approximately $50,000 a year to supplement their Social Security income and maintain their pre-retirement lifestyle. Since they have a portfolio of $1.5 million, they figure they can safely withdraw that amount, but they also want to keep their tax rate as low as possible.

Fortunately, John has $120,000 in a Roth IRA and Sarah's Roth is worth $135,000. By tapping those funds first, John and Sarah can realize up to $36,000 in tax-free income in the coming year, and they will need to generate only $14,000 more from their taxable accounts. That should keep their tax bracket low, far lower than when they were still working.

Keep in mind that I don't always recommend tapping into non-retirement accounts first before taking required minimum distributions (RMDs) from retirement accounts. Many advisors do recommend this, with the logic being that you should delay paying taxes for as long as possible, or minimize them for as long as possible. Withdrawals from a Roth IRA are tax-free and withdrawals from non-retirement investment accounts are taxed at the capital gains rate, which is generally less than the rate on ordinary income.

The reason I deviate from some of my colleagues is that when you're left with nothing but retirement accounts and your withdrawals are taxed as ordinary income, any time you must make a large withdrawal for an emergency or a large purchase, you risk moving up into a higher income tax bracket. If you needed to make a $30,000 repair on your home, for example, you might have to withdraw approximately *$50,000* to cover the taxes. This is because the $30,000 would be taxed in the 40% range or higher—and you'd have to pay taxes on the money you withdraw to cover the taxes!

If you retain funds in a Roth, there is no tax hit. If the funds are in a non-retirement account, the tax hit is often less severe when you have to make that big withdrawal because you're only paying long-term capital gains taxes instead of taxes on ordinary income. (The tax rates on long-term capital gains are significantly less for most income brackets.)

The Impact of Capital Gains Taxes

This brings me to my next tax tip: One of the best ways to lower your taxable income is to minimize your capital gains. Capital gains may be taxed at a lower rate than ordinary income, but with the implementation of the Affordable Care Act, also known as Obamacare, high earners are now subject to an additional tax on their capital gains. If you're fortunate enough to be a high earner, this gives you one more incentive to keep those gains as low as possible.

Trading stocks and mutual funds frequently opens you up to high capital gains taxes. Short-term capital gains (profits on securities held for exactly one year or less) are taxed at your top marginal tax rate. If you are a long-term investor, you can reduce your capital gains exposure significantly because long-term gains are taxed at a lower rate. Considering the lesson from the chapter on return on behavior, in my view, being a long-term investor is a no-brainer: better returns in the long run with far lower taxes.

Tax-loss harvesting is another smart way to reduce your capital gains taxes and lower your total tax bill. In a perfect world, every investment would work out exactly as you intended, and every stock and mutual fund you bought would appreciate in value. In the real world, however, even the savviest investor will see their portfolio lose value at some point.

Tax-loss harvesting allows you to turn those investment losses into tax savings. You can write off up to $3,000 of losses against your capital gains, reducing the amount of those gains and reducing your tax bill in the process. Better yet, if your tax losses exceed your current-year capital gains, you can roll the loss forward into future years. That means you can benefit from the results of that bad investment year after year. Note that if you have a short-term capital gain, it may only be offset by a short-term capital loss.

Saving for Retirement—and Saving on Your Taxes

You probably already know that you can also save a substantial amount on your tax bill by making smart use of retirement saving plans. If you work for a for-profit employer, enrolling in the company 401(k) plan can sharply reduce your taxable income and the amount on which you pay taxes. If you are fifty years of age or older, maxing out your 401(k) plan contribution could reduce your taxable income by nearly $20,000. Even if you are younger than fifty, you can save more than $15,000 for retirement and reduce your taxable income by the same amount.

If you work for a nonprofit agency or a school, you may be able to reduce your taxable income by participating in their 403(b) plan. The basic concept is the same, as is the amount of money you can set aside.

No matter who you work for, checking with your human resources department and signing up for their retirement plan could save you a ton of money, not only this year but all the way out to retirement.

You can save even more by taking advantage of IRA contributions. A traditional IRA allows you to take a tax deduction now, reducing your taxable income and helping you save for retirement. In exchange for the up-front tax deduction, you pay taxes when you withdraw the funds in retirement. In the meantime, you enjoy years' worth of investment returns and appreciation, all the while sheltering those funds from the taxman. Note that if you already have a 401(k), the amount you contribute to that account in a given year may affect the amount of tax savings you get from the traditional IRA.

A traditional IRA can be a great choice for workers in a high tax bracket. If you are in the highest tax bracket, reducing your taxable income now can save you a significant amount of money. If your tax bracket is lower, you may benefit more from a Roth IRA. In my opinion, Roth IRA accounts are an underutilized financial planning tool.

When you contribute money to a Roth IRA, you give up the up-front tax benefit you would have gotten with a traditional account. You pay taxes on the income you contribute to the Roth just as you would pay taxes on income you spent on a vacation. In exchange, however, you get to enjoy tax-free withdrawals in retirement. That makes a Roth IRA the perfect choice for workers who are in a low tax bracket now. Since your current tax rate is low, the value you would get from a traditional IRA is somewhat limited. On the other hand, the benefit of withdrawing appreciated assets tax-free in retirement holds great appeal.

A Roth IRA is also a great choice for workers who believe they will be in a higher tax bracket in retirement than they are now. If, for instance, you are eligible for a significant company pension and already have a lot of financial assets, your postretirement income could be higher than what you make now. That makes a Roth IRA a great deal, since you can draw on those funds first and keep your taxable income—and your tax bill—low in your retirement years.

Similarly, if you believe that tax rates will rise in the decades to come—a safe assumption in these days of runaway debt and dysfunctional government—you can use a Roth IRA to mitigate your risks and blunt the effects of those higher taxes. Having part of your retirement nest egg in a tax-free vehicle like a Roth IRA makes a lot of sense, whether or not taxes rise in the years leading up to your retirement.

If your spouse works, he or she may also be eligible to contribute to a traditional or Roth IRA. Eligibility for a traditional or Roth IRA depends on the combined income of you and your spouse, so you should always check with your accountant or tax expert before making any contributions. If your spouse is eligible for an IRA based on his or her income, the amount you contribute will further reduce your combined taxable income and help you save even more.

Even if your spouse is not employed, you may still be able to contribute to a spousal IRA based on your own income. Again, it is important to check with your tax expert or accountant to determine eligibility and find out how much you can save.

Reducing Income Taxes for Business Owners

There are also plenty of ways to reduce your taxable income if you are a business owner. There has been a lot of talk about lowering tax rates for small business owners, but until Congress actually does something, you need to take charge of the situation and do what you can to lower your own tax rate.

If you are self-employed or own your own business, you have a number of retirement-saving and tax-lowering vehicles at your disposal. A SEP-IRA is an excellent choice for sole proprietors and small business owners, as is its cousin, the SIMPLE IRA. Both retirement plans have generous contribution limits, and that translates into a lower taxable income for your business and a much lower tax bill.

Business owners can save even more through the use of a Solo 401(k), also known as an Individual 401(k). No matter what it is called, this retirement savings plan functions much the same as a traditional IRA, but it is designed for sole proprietors and self-employed business owners. The contribution limits for a Solo 401(k) are higher those of either a SEP-IRA or SIMPLE IRA, but there are also some additional reporting rules you will need to follow. If you want to maximize the amount you put aside for retirement and the amount you reduce your taxable income, it is hard to beat a Solo 401(k).

Investing in, and for, the Future

If your financial plan includes saving for the education of your children, you can take advantage of a 529 plan. While the contributions you make to a 529 plan are not tax deductible, the amount you contribute grows and compounds tax-free, until it is withdrawn to pay for educational expenses.

If your children are young, with more than a decade to go before college, the value of those compounded tax-free earnings can be quite significant, making a 529 plan one of the best college-saving vehicles out there.

Even if your kids have a shorter time horizon, opening and contributing to a 529 plan will probably be worthwhile. The sooner you get started, the more valuable the plan can be; but every dollar you save now is one less dollar you will have to pay later. College costs are going nowhere but up, and putting today's dollars away now can have a huge impact when your child is ready to enter college in the future.

Reducing your taxable income now and saving money on your taxes is important, but you also need to look out for the next generation. As a parent, and possibly a grandparent, you have worked hard to set your children, and grandchildren, up for success. You have contributed to their 529 plans and reaped the tax-free earnings those plans provided. You have provided them with a sound financial education, from teaching them how to balance a checkbook to giving them the basics on mutual funds and the stock market. Now that your offspring have graduated from college and started families of their own, it is time to give them one final gift.

The right estate plan can make a huge difference in the financial security of the next generation, and it is never too early to get started. Proper estate planning starts with a will, but a will alone is not enough to protect your heirs from confiscatory estate taxes.

Having an estate plan in place can reduce the financial burden on your children and grandchildren and let them inherit the nest egg you worked so hard to accumulate. Estate planning should be an integral part of your financial planning strategy, and you should not treat it as a mere afterthought.

It is always best to have your entire financial planning team—from your certified financial planner and your accountant to your tax expert and your estate planning attorney—work together. Making sure that everyone is on the right page is the best way to maximize the value of each service and ensure you (and your heirs) keep as much of every dollar you earn as possible.

Advanced Strategies for Tax Minimization

As you can see, opportunities for minimizing your taxable income and reducing your tax bill exist for just about everyone. From contributing to your 401(k) plan at work to being smart about how you invest in the stock market, there are lots of things you can do to make your taxes less taxing.

If you want to save even more, there are advanced tax-saving strategies you can employ. For instance, if you own a mutual fund or ETF that has lost money since you bought it but you still believe it's a solid long-term investment based on fundamentals, you can actually harvest your loss and still retain your position. That way, if the fund does turn around, you can enjoy the benefit. At the same time, you can take the tax loss now and reduce your taxable income and your current tax bill.

It works like this: You sell the money-losing fund or ETF, then purchase a different fund or ETF (one that's the same asset class, similar composition, but different issuer) right away. You get to stay in the same type of investment, and this shift in assets is not subject to the "wash-sale" rule. That rule prohibits you from selling an investment at a loss and buying it back within thirty days.

If you choose to implement this tax-saving strategy, you should always seek advice from your accountant or tax expert. Determining which investments are, and are not, subject to the wash-sale rule can be a complicated matter, and you do not want to make a costly mistake.

If you are already in retirement, you can further reduce your tax bill and your taxable income by implementing a smart withdrawal strategy. Simply changing the balance of withdrawals from your taxable and tax-free accounts could substantially reduce your income for the year and keep your tax bill to a minimum.

For instance, if you have a high amount of capital gains this year due to a large sale of stock, you could pull the additional income you need from your tax-free Roth IRA, rather than tapping the taxable money in your traditional one. This kind of balancing act can keep your taxes low and help you make the most of your nest egg down the line.

Health Care Tax Strategies

No matter where you are in the retirement-planning process, you can bet that health care expenses will play a major role in your future and in the future of your spouse and loved ones. Health care and health insurance costs continue to rise higher than the rate of inflation, and there is no reason to believe that trend will not continue. Whether you are still working or already in retirement, you need to look for ways to lower the cost of health insurance and keep more money in your pocket.

One of the best strategies for both current workers and early retirees is to choose a health insurance plan with a high deductible. That high deductible may seem daunting, but keep in mind that it comes with lower monthly premiums. Those lower monthly premiums can more than make up for the potential of higher costs if you get sick, especially if you and your spouse are still relatively healthy.

You can maximize the benefit of a high-deductible health plan by pairing it with a health savings account (HSA). A health savings account allows you to put money aside now for future health care expenses—and enjoy a healthy up-front tax break in the process.

The money you put into your HSA is allowed to grow and compound over time, making the investment that much more valuable in the future. If you do not use all of your HSA for health care expenses, you can even put the money toward the cost of a Medicare supplement plan after you retire and become eligible for the government-sponsored health care plan.

Contributing to a health savings account can be particularly advantageous for self-employed individuals and business owners, but it is also a smart tax move for ordinary workers. More and more employers are recognizing the inherent value of high-deductible health plans and health savings accounts, and many are offering this option to their employees. If your company offers such a plan, you should definitely take a good look at its potential benefits.

Please note that you are only eligible for an HSA if you are enrolled in a high-deductible plan, you are not enrolled in Medicare, and you have no other conflicting health coverage. The IRS website is actually a great resource for the "other health coverage" that is permitted for those who want to enroll in an HSA.

If you are self-employed or your employer does not offer an HSA, many banks do offer these types of accounts. In addition, your financial advisor may also be able to open an HSA for you as well.

Stretch Your Retirement Savings with a Stretch IRA

If you want to make your retirement savings plan even more valuable, consider converting some of your assets to a stretch IRA as part of your estate planning process. A stretch IRA allows your designated heirs, typically your children, to inherit your IRA and take the money out based on their life expectancy instead of yours.

That simple change can sharply reduce the recipient's tax bill and give the IRA assets more time to grow and compound. Incorporating a stretch IRA into your estate planning is a great way to give your children one final gift—one that they can rely on for the rest of their lives.

Retirees have far more leeway when it comes to taking income and paying taxes. By shifting investments into tax-free buckets and putting off the sale of stocks and mutual funds, retirees are better able to control how much they earn, and how much they ship off to Washington when April 15 rolls around.

One of the best ways to control your tax bracket and minimize the amount you send to Uncle Sam is to have a diversified set of accounts you can draw from. Maintaining a traditional IRA, a Roth IRA, and a number of personal taxable accounts gives you a great degree of flexibility and allows you to stay in the lowest tax bracket possible.

Leaving a Financial Legacy to Your Loved Ones

"We should not forget that it will be just as important to our descendants to be prosperous in their time as it is to us to be prosperous in our time."

–THEODORE ROOSEVELT

FOR MANY INVESTORS, accumulating enough wealth to achieve financial independence isn't enough. Leaving a legacy to loved ones is just as vital for their financial peace of mind. It's one final gift to be remembered by and one more way to make sure the people you care about will be all right.

There are two distinct components to planning and leaving a financial legacy, and we will examine each of those two components individually. The first part of the financial legacy equation is making sure you are on track to provide the size inheritance you want to leave behind. This requires planning and preparation, as the nest egg you have established will also need to produce enough income for you to live your lifestyle after you stop working. Leaving a legacy to your loved ones is important, but it should not come at the expense of your own financial security.

Your spending is a big component to leaving a legacy. If your spending is sustainable and your assets have been able to grow with rising prices, you are on track to live a comfortable life in retirement and leave a substantial inheritance.

If, on the other hand, you find yourself withdrawing more from your portfolio than it's growing, you may need to rethink the legacy you're leaving behind. Do not forget that the most important legacy you can leave your children is your care, compassion, and love. Money is great, but it cannot replace the gift of knowledge and teaching you have already been able to pass on to your children and grandchildren.

The first part of leaving a financial legacy for your loved ones is making sure you are on track. If an examination of your finances shows that you are on track, the next step is to make sure that all of your documents are up to date and that they are able to accomplish the things you want.

Do you have a fully executed will and a plan for avoiding probate? Are you working with a professional estate planning attorney? Do you understand the challenges your heirs could face if things are not handled correctly? Until you can answer those questions, your estate planning is not complete.

Let's take a look at an estate planning cautionary tale that I think illustrates how critical proper estate planning really is. Jane and Steven married late in life, and it was the second marriage for each of them. Jane had two grown children who were out on their own and doing great. After several years of marriage, she and Steven had a child of their own, a daughter who was born with special needs. Steven and Jane had been planning to update their wills, but with the challenges of taking care of a special-needs daughter, they simply never got around to it.

When Steven and Jane died in a tragic car crash, their infant daughter was left all alone, and because the old will was still in force, their assets were passed down to Jane's two grown children. Luckily for their half-sibling, those kids stepped up and did the right thing, using the funds to care for the child. The situation could have been avoided with a single trip to a good estate planning attorney. And it could have been far worse: Jane's children were under no legal obligation to step up and care for their half-sister. Imagine what might have happened to the child had they been less generous people!

The Three Critical Questions You Must Ask Yourself

Before you take another step down the estate planning road or even think about leaving a financial legacy to your loved ones, ask yourself three critical questions:

- What are my legacy goals?

- How do I prioritize my legacy goals against my current lifestyle goals?

- What level of certainty do I need in order to have peace of mind?

For some people, leaving a legacy could be as simple as naming an only child the beneficiary of an IRA account. For others, the goals could be extremely complicated, involving everything from special-needs children, to the distribution of assets to children and grandchildren from multiple marriages, to business-continuity planning for the self-employed. No matter how simple or complicated your legacy goals are, it is important to set them down in writing. Until you know what your goals are, even the most dedicated plan will not get you there.

Now it is time to look at priorities, and that means thinking long and hard about how important each goal is. You obviously want to leave a legacy for your loved ones, but are you willing (or able) to sacrifice your current wants and needs to do that?

Even the wealthiest individual has only a limited number of dollars, and spending a dollar here means it will not be available there. If you put an extra dollar into a growth account earmarked for your loved ones and their legacy, that is one less dollar you have to enjoy a great vacation or make a down payment on your next new car.

The third and final question you need to ask yourself concerns certainty versus flexibility, something that every investor is familiar with. Would you rather have the peace of mind that comes with a safe, low-risk investment or insurance product even if you're getting a much lower expected rate of return? Or can you live with more volatility, and perhaps more flexibility and liquidity, in exchange for a higher expected return? The answers to these questions are very important, and you need to think carefully about them.

Remember, you don't have to retain the same level of certainty and risk forever. In your fifties, if you have funds earmarked for an inheritance, you may want to invest in assets with higher expected returns, with more flexibility and less certainty. Knowing a single financial storm can dramatically reduce the amount your heirs get, as you transition into your golden years, you may want less risk and more certainty for peace of mind.

Fortunately, there are some strategies you can use to reduce uncertainty and build flexibility into your legacy plan. You can, for instance, use life insurance as part of your estate planning, making it easier to pass your wealth to your heirs without paying unnecessary taxes or complicating the inheritance process.

You can also use a trust to benefit your heirs, once again passing on your nest egg while avoiding unnecessary taxes and relieving the strain at the difficult time of your passing. When executed properly, a trust may also help heirs avoid the costs and potential stresses of probate.

No matter what kind of strategy you use, it is important to lay out your wishes, put them in writing, and have them prepared or reviewed by an experienced estate planning attorney who understands your goals. Your financial planner should be involved as well. The planners at my firm frequently make introductions to estate planning attorneys and sit in on the meetings to ensure everyone is on the same page.

Using Life Insurance as a Planning Tool

Let's take a more in-depth look at how life insurance can aid your plan to leave a legacy for your loved ones. Let's look at the hypothetical example of a couple, Jack and Janet, who were able to accumulate an impressive $4 million nest egg over a lifetime of hard work, dedication, and planning. Since their $4 million nest egg makes estate taxes a consideration, they decided to use life insurance to make it easier to pass their wealth along to their heirs. Insurance, of course, is a high-certainty, low-flexibility option.

Jack and Janet know that the proceeds of a life insurance policy are generally tax-free to the recipients. What they did not know, however, is that there are important exceptions to that tax-free rule. Fortunately, their estate planning attorney was able to outline the circumstances in which life insurance proceeds could be taxable and help Jack and Janet avoid them.

There are three circumstances under which the proceeds of a life insurance policy could be taxable, including if the proceeds of the policy are paid to the executor of the decedent's estate or if the deceased individuals possessed an incident of ownership in the policy.

Due to the IRS's three-year rule, proceeds of the life insurance policy may also be taxable if there was a transfer of ownership for the policy within the three years prior to the death of the policyholder. That three-year rule is very important, and that is why it is important to work with an experienced financial planner and estate planning attorney. Fortunately for Jack and Janet, they had the help of such a team, and they were able to use life insurance to create a substantial financial legacy for their loved ones in a tax-efficient way.

Using life insurance to build a financial legacy for your loved ones is one strategy, but it is not the only one. There are other, more flexible ways to pass on wealth to the next generation and help the ones you love enjoy a more financially successful future when you pass on.

Using Retirement Accounts to Pass On a Financial Legacy

The same tools you use to plan your own retirement income, namely your 401(k) plan and your IRA, can also serve as the foundation of your financial legacy. Leaving your assets in standard accounts like an IRA or 401(k) plan provides you with additional flexibility and gives you the freedom to spend the proceeds in any way you see fit.

You can, for instance, use the money in your IRA or 401(k) to provide current income in your retirement years, drawing on the funds as needed and taking your required minimum distribution (RMD) each year. At the same time, the money you do not tap continues to grow, building wealth for your future and serving as the basis for the financial legacy you will one day leave behind.

Spousal heirs who inherit a 401(k) or IRA are required to take RMDs each year once the late spouse would have been 70.5 years old. Non-spousal heirs such as children or grandchildren have more flexibility: They can take the entire amount all at once (potentially taking on a big tax hit), take the RMD each year over time (the younger the heir, the lower the RMD; it's not based on the original owner's age), or take the inheritance over five years.

The decision to take it all at once, as an RMD, or over five years will impact tax liabilities; non-spousal inheritance counts as taxable income. While this isn't a fun topic to discuss at Thanksgiving dinner, family communication about these matters is key to helping your children get the most out of what you leave behind. It's also wise to leave a letter behind with your intentions; for example, if you want to implement a stretch IRA, designating your youngest child as the beneficiary because the RMD will be the smallest for the youngest (and hence, the total taxes paid may be the smallest), make sure they know why you want that to happen, how it should be implemented (by retitling the current IRA rather than transferring to another account or institution), and any other wishes.

Factors That Can Impact Your Ability to Leave a Financial Legacy

There are a number of factors that can impact your ability to pass on a financial legacy to your loved ones, or at least the size of the legacy you will eventually leave behind. Again, we will take a look at some important questions you need to ask yourself.

The first question is how much money you can safely spend each year without adversely affecting your goals. Can you, for instance, withdraw enough extra income to enjoy a wonderful annual vacation and still be able to pass on the amount you planned to leave your children?

If the answer to that question is yes, you do not have to do a thing. Just withdraw that ten grand from your portfolio—from the most tax-efficient account—and head off to Europe, Asia, Africa, or anywhere else you want to go.

If the answer is no, or maybe, you have some more work to do. You may need to take another look at your priorities and weigh the current enjoyment you can receive from your nest egg against the size of the financial legacy you want to leave for your loved ones.

The second question you need to ask yourself is how much risk you are able to accept. Your retirement years, of course, are a time to minimize and balance risks. You don't want a single-day stock market correction of 25% to force you into selling low in order to have the cash you need to live your lifestyle. You should at least have enough money in your short-term, low-risk bucket to avoid that.

Keep in mind that in some circumstances, playing it too safe can be just as dangerous to your future financial legacy as taking on too much risk. Keeping your entire nest egg in safe investments like bank CDs and government bonds could mean that your return does not keep pace with rising prices and taxes. This may cause you to draw down your portfolio too quickly and reduce the amount left over at the end of your journey.

There is no doubt that answering these questions involves a delicate balancing act, so it is important to choose the financial products that best align with the level of certainty or flexibility you want and need. These delicate subjects are the ones where it's really invaluable to be working with a Certified Financial Planner who will listen to you and make your goals his or her top priority when giving advice. There's no single right answer that fits everyone. It's your decision; and in order to make a good one, you may need to speak with someone who can clearly articulate the pros and cons of each of your options—the risks and potential rewards—and who understands the human element of needing financial peace of mind.

Are You on Track to Achieve Your Legacy Goals?

No matter where you are on the road to leaving a lasting financial legacy for your loved ones, it is important to take a step back once in a while and make sure you are still on track. In many cases, a few small adjustments may be all it takes to get your legacy goals back on track and give you confidence that you will be able to pass on your assets to your loved ones in the manner you envision.

Many firms offer a highly useful tool to help you assess the status of your financial legacy and give you added peace of mind. Our retirement income analysis stress-tests your financial assets relative to their ability to fund all of your goals. It simulates 1,000 economic scenarios and the impacts they may have on your income streams and on your portfolio, and then gives you your probability of success. If, for example, you are able to fund all of your goals in 820 out of 1,000 scenarios, you have an 82% probability of success.

This assessment can be extremely valuable, particularly when you plug in the amount of money you would like to spend each year to live your lifestyle in addition to the size of the financial legacy you'd like to leave behind. You can then see how adjusting your legacy goals up or down, or increasing or decreasing the cost of your lifestyle, impacts your probability of success. You can change your goal(s) and instantly see how that impacts the probability of success. You can also change your assumptions, like the amount you contribute to your investment accounts each month, and see how each change impacts your current retirement goals and the long-term financial legacy you hope to leave for your loved ones.

You may find that simply increasing the amount of your biweekly 401(k) plan contribution is enough to get your financial legacy goals back on track. On the other hand, you may find that the level of sacrifice you would need to make to meet your goal of a substantial financial legacy is simply not realistic. In that case, you may need to look at other ways to leave a legacy for those you care about.

Leaving a Nonfinancial Legacy

Remember, leaving a lump sum of cash is only one way to establish a lasting financial legacy for those you love. For instance, helping to finance the education of your children or grandchildren can be a much better—and longer-lasting—financial legacy than leaving a substantial nest egg.

Let's take a look at two hypothetical scenarios. The names are made up, but the events described are all too real. In fact, you probably know a few families who fall into one category or the other.

Our first couple, Mike and Julie, worked all their lives to build a business and pass on a financial legacy to their children. They raised great kids and added to their college funds from the day they were born, but they still insisted that their two children pay for part of their educations.

When the time came, their kids went off to college and worked through the summers to put themselves through school and prepare for the future. Today, Mike and Julie's son, Mark, is an engineer, and their daughter, Jennifer, is a successful doctor. Mike and Julie, meanwhile, are enjoying the fruits of a well-planned retirement, traveling extensively and spending lavishly on gifts for their grandchildren. When they eventually pass on, there may not be a huge nest egg remaining, but their legacy will live on in the successful lives their children have been able to build for themselves.

Now let's look at the other end of the spectrum, an extremely wealthy couple we will call Bill and Melissa. Bill and Melissa were also quite successful in business, and they have built a substantial nest egg to pass on to their children. Unfortunately, their children are not as responsible, or as well equipped, as young Mark and Jennifer.

Their kids, let's call them Alan and Claire, were raised in the lap of luxury, enjoying a lifestyle that those born into lesser financial circumstances could never imagine. From a multimillion-dollar home to brand new sports cars for their sixteenth birthdays, their parents made sure that young Alan and Claire never wanted for anything.

When Bill and Melissa passed on, they left their offspring an impressive portfolio of investments, along with business interests well into the eight figures. That multimillion-dollar nest egg was not enough, however, because the children never learned personal finance and the value of money.

I don't bring this up to preach on parenting, but more as a reminder that it's okay to put your goals and desired lifestyle first.

You've done your job as a parent, worked hard all your life, and in almost all cases your heirs would probably be willing to inherit a little less in exchange for knowing you were able to fulfill your own personal dreams.

Financial Planning for Family Members with Special Needs

Leaving a financial legacy for your loved ones can be a complicated matter, but things become even harder when those loved ones have special needs. Whether you are dealing with a child who was born with a severe birth defect, a sibling with a chronic illness that renders them unable to work and earn a living, or a son or daughter who suffered a debilitating illness or accident later in life, the presence of these special needs makes a lasting financial legacy all the more important.

A quick glance at the statistics surrounding families with special needs shows both the importance of sound financial planning and how far we have to go. A recent survey of families with special-needs children found that nearly 70% do not have a will, more than half have not identified a guardian, and more than 70% have not named a trustee.

Perhaps not surprisingly, nearly 90% have not yet created a special-needs trust for their children, and nearly 85% do not even have a written letter of intent in place. All of these things are very important, and it is never too early to start planning.

If your family includes those with special needs, there are a number of documents you absolutely must have in place. These critical documents will form the backbone of your estate planning process: a last will and testament, general durable powers of attorney for financial affairs, a durable medical power of attorney, a revocable living trust, a supplemental special needs trust, and a letter of intent. If your estate plan does not currently include all of these documents, make an appointment with an estate planning attorney right away.

Estate Planning Options for Families with Special Needs

Families who have loved ones with special needs have a number of options when it comes to estate planning and the distribution of assets. They can distribute their assets outright to their special needs children; however, depending on the degree of disability, that may not be recommended.

Distributing assets outright to a special needs individual may render the individual ineligible for important government benefits, which are often based on needs and available assets. In the end, the direct distribution of assets to an individual with special needs can be counterproductive. Fortunately, there are other, and better, options available for families with special-needs children.

It is also not recommended to disinherit a special-needs child, since doing so would leave the vulnerable individual without a safety net or any means of support if government benefits were cut or eliminated in the future.

Additional estate planning options include leaving property to another family member with the understanding that the assets will be used for the care of the special-needs child. That arrangement is also not typically recommended, since this kind of informal agreement is not legally enforceable.

That is why many families choose to establish a third-party supplemental needs trust for the special-needs child. This is typically the most highly recommended option, since the presence of the trust will not disqualify the special-needs child from important governmental benefits or support programs.

As you can see, estate planning becomes a great deal more complicated when dealing with family members who have special needs. Those special-needs individuals may rely on you, your guidance, and your income to meet their daily needs and make their way in life. In your absence, you will have to leave behind a financial legacy that takes their special needs into account and provides the support they will need to carry on for the rest of their lives.

Estate planning may not be a fun thing to think about. After all, the very fact that you are planning your estate means you are acknowledging that you will die one day. Even if that date is decades in the future, coming face to face with your own mortality is not exactly something most people look forward to.

But no matter how unpleasant, establishing an estate plan and financial legacy for your loved ones is very important, if for no other reason than it's probably important to you. It's 18% of the Lifestyle Sustainability Scorecard for this reason—with 8% weighting on whether you're on track and 10% on whether your estate documents are up to date. (Even if you don't care about leaving a legacy at the end of the long road, I'm sure you agree that it's best to have things in order in case the journey gets cut short unexpectedly.)

If you have not yet started your estate planning or given much thought to the financial legacy you will leave your loved ones, now is the perfect time to begin. Whether you work with your current financial planner or hire an estate planning attorney to get you started, the time to start planning is now.

The Most Important Investment You'll Ever Make

THROUGHOUT THIS BOOK, I have shared with you the financial planning and investment strategies critical to achieving and sustaining *your* idea of true wealth. I have introduced you to my firm's Lifestyle Sustainability Scorecard™ and how it may be used to eliminate your financial worries by addressing the fifteen critical risks that have the potential to derail your family's lifestyle—or, at the very least, impede your ability to achieve and sustain your goals. You've also learned specific strategies to address these risks, as well as some high-level philosophies to guide your financial problem solving.

Along the way, I have shared both financial success stories and cautionary tales with the goal of highlighting a core belief of mine: That your money is more than just numbers; it also touches nearly every aspect of your emotional life as well. True wealth isn't about acquiring things. It's about financial independence and peace of mind. It's about being able to confidently answer questions such as—

- Is your family's income protected from unexpected injury, illness, or premature death?

- Will you be able to generate enough income to sustain your lifestyle through financial storms?

- Will your retirement income sustain the lifestyle your family deserves despite the ravages of rising prices and taxes?

- Do you have a proper estate plan in place to ensure a smooth and tax-efficient transfer of wealth at the end of the road?

- Do you have a solid strategy to avoid becoming a burden to your loved ones when you get older and potentially require long-term care?

- Do you have the right level of guaranteed income and asset diversification to smooth out returns so that you avoid the behavioral mistakes that prevent most investors from getting the returns they deserve?

These are questions that must be answered in order to feel truly confident in your financial future and be able to go to sleep at night without worrying about money.

My Final Investment Tip

Now that our journey is nearly at an end, it is time to take a look at one more investment that I touched upon only briefly in the chapter on maximizing your income capability. However, this is arguably the most important investment you will ever make. The investment I speak of here is the investment in yourself—in your education, your career, your base of knowledge, whom you turn to for advice, and how you allocate your most precious and scarce resource: your time.

Be a Financial Co-Pilot with Your Advisor

One trend I have noticed and embraced is that as investors have become more sophisticated in their knowledge of financial markets, they have understandably become more hands-on in their financial planning. Fewer clients than ever before simply want to delegate all of their "financial stuff" to a professional planner. They still turn to advisors for specialization and expertise, but nowadays they tend to show up to first appointments with ideas of their own.

Investors today often form opinions about the advice given to them, rather than defer. I think it's a wise choice to insist on being a co-pilot with your advisor. If something conflicts with your common sense or existing belief, challenge it. Your advisor's role in the relationship should be not only to advise you but also to communicate effectively until you are comfortable with the path forward.

My hope is that you use what you've learned in this book to co-pilot your financial planning along with your advisor. Many financial advisors—even those with the Certified Financial Planner designation—focus almost exclusively on investing strategies and selling insurance. To be fair, many of them would prefer to do more planning for clients but have found it difficult to build a profitable business around it. As co-pilot, mention the risks on the Lifestyle Sustainability Scorecard™ to your advisor and ask for advice on how to address them. The right advisor will be thrilled to help. When you get advice on these topics, ask your advisor to disclose any conflicts of interest and how he or she gets paid for any insurance products or investments they recommend.

Here are a few other ways to adopt the co-pilot mindset with your advisor:

- Ask for the rationale behind the securities funds they recommend, the other options considered, and why the final recommendations were the best options for them.

- Request a stress test on your assets to see how another Great Recession may impact your lifestyle sustainability.

- Initiate a conversation about the best way to generate predictable streams of income that keep pace with rising prices and taxes.

- Discuss the types of accounts you should own, the order from which you should withdraw, and the short- and long-term tax consequences of various options.

- At the end of the year, check your portfolio performance and call your advisor to discuss any tax-loss harvesting opportunities.

- Schedule a time for you and your estate attorney, tax accountant, and financial planner to meet regarding tax-efficient transfers of assets to heirs.

- Talk to your advisor about when and how to claim Social Security and Medicare, the impact of your choices on the surviving spouse, and how your various options address longevity risk (the risk of outliving your assets).

Obviously, I highly recommend working with an advisor who is proactive and does not require prodding on these critical topics. However, even the best of advisors are human, and *nobody* cares about your money as much as you do!

Invest in Yourself Beyond Financial Planning Tactics

You can probably tell by now simply from the assumptions I use throughout this book, such as 6% average annual returns in your portfolio, that I don't believe in "getting rich" from great stock picking. Choosing right can certainly pay off, and as you know I'm a big proponent of letting your money work hard for you through the magic of compound earnings. However, that is only one piece of the wealth puzzle.

In chapter four, I gave the example of a solopreneur attorney who faced a decision to continue earning a good living as a practitioner or reinvest in his firm and become an entrepreneurial attorney who would go on to build a firm with much higher income potential. Of course, the decision to pursue the latter path comes with additional risk. To build a firm, the attorney had to briefly suspend his retirement contribution—something I almost never advocate—and there was always the possibility that his investment would fail to produce the additional income he desired. However, the long-term upside for him is also far greater than if he remained a solo act.

Increasing your income—whether it's a salary increase or higher business profits—opens so many opportunities. In addition to simply having more money short-term, it allows you to invest more each year and put even more money to work for you through compound earnings. It may have an exponential effect on your wealth in that way. Additional income also allows you to build an emergency fund faster, ensure your family's security further, and potentially even retire earlier.

Oftentimes an investment in oneself is required to make this type of substantial leap in income. Your investment may be monetary—such as this example of reinvesting in your business; an investment of your time—for example working longer hours early in your career; or an investment of both—such as a college education or even informal training.

Warren Buffett has long stressed the importance of investing in your personal capital, as have many other successful entrepreneurs and business owners. From Jeff Bezos at Amazon.com and Mark Zuckerberg at Facebook to Henry Ford and Bill Gates, the most successful and influential people in the world have been preaching the value of self-investment for centuries.

In many ways, investing in yourself is not much different from investing in stocks, bonds, mutual funds, and the like. Whether you are investing in yourself, your business, or the stock market, it always pays to take the long view. Instead of going for the short-term score or looking for that get-rich-quick scheme, investing in yourself is a long-term process, one with many steps on the road to success.

The Investment in Education

The key questions you need to ask yourself when choosing a college, either for yourself or helping your child, are: What is your passion, and what is your expected return on investment?

In my opinion, it's critical for students to choose a college that supports their passion: If someone has his or her heart set on studying psychology, finding a school with a strong psychology department is the best way to feed that passion and get the most out of college. Attending a school based on the student's passion is also the best way to avoid changing majors midstream—a costly mistake too many students make these days. The ideal time to find your passion is before you enter college, not after.

Many students choose a "practical" major instead of their passion, or they choose a major based on what someone else wants for them rather than what they want for themselves. The reasons may often be logical, but it's also a recipe to suffer from burnout and be unhappy. Even if the student manages to slog through college studying a topic that isn't a good fit, he or she now has a fifty-year working career to get through.

Needless to say, it's hard to enjoy a life of true wealth and happiness doing something you're not passionate about *for five decades*.

I admit that the financial return on a college investment is also important. You should not invest in an asset class without past evidence supporting the investment, so why would you spend hundreds of thousands of dollars on higher education without knowing how other students have fared financially after graduation? Are a significant percentage of graduates working in their chosen field? What are their salaries? How many have started their own businesses? The answers to these questions can help you understand the return on investment you can expect from the college you are considering.

Graduating from college with a mountain of debt you can't afford to pay back is not a great investment in yourself, even if you enjoyed the four years.

Investing in Yourself Beyond College

Please allow me to indulge myself here and use my own experience as an example. As this book comes to an end, I believe it is appropriate to share my personal journey and explain how making an investment in my own future has benefited me, my clients, and my financial position.

From the very beginning of my career, investing in my own continuing education and building my firm has proven to be the best move I ever made.

I started by own financial advisory firm back in 1985, right after graduating from college. I became a Certified Financial Planner in 1988, and since then I have grown my firm substantially from its humble beginnings. The firm I started in 1985 now has more than $450 million in assets under management.

Throughout my personal journey, the investments I have made in myself, my business, and my team have been a huge part of my success. We have improved our investing and financial planning strategies by going beyond our continued education requirements. We obtain certifications in specialized areas of personal finance, such as special-needs planning or divorce planning. We subscribe to in-depth research reports like DALBAR's Quantitative Analysis of Investor Behavior, and enhance our advisory capabilities by adapting new technology.

Of course, my firm's value—both in terms of market share and in terms of the value we add for clients—has grown substantially as we have hired new talent, with diverse backgrounds and specialties, and then reinvested in the team by learning even more together. I would not be where I am today without surrounding myself with such immense talent.

Investing in Yourself by Preparing for Disruptive Technologies

Try to think back to 1996. Bill Clinton was running for reelection, and we were getting ready for the new millennium and the coming end of the world (remember Y2K?). There were no iPhones, no social media, and no commercially available hybrid cars, let alone a Toyota Prius that could drive itself.

Back then a company you probably grew up with called Kodak employed more than 140,000 people around the world, and the company had a market capitalization of roughly $24 billion. Whether you were a weekend shutterbug or a professional photographer, you knew the Kodak name and used its products. When you bought film (remember film?) at the local store, chances are it was Kodak film. When you had your prints developed, they were probably printed on Kodak paper. Kodak was the undisputed leader in the world of photography, and the executives of the company thought that would never change.

Then the digital revolution caught Kodak flat-footed. Kodak failed to respond to the disruptive technology of digital cameras, and in 2012 the company filed for Chapter 11 bankruptcy. As of 2015, the company had only 6,400 employees remaining.

Disruptive technologies have ended many businesses and careers while creating new ones over the past twenty years. This is called creative destruction, and it's both necessary and brutal. Necessary because it drives us forward, and brutal because it's unforgiving.

I will not prognosticate on the disruptive technologies that will both create and destroy businesses and careers in the future, but I strongly encourage everyone to invest in themselves with this force in mind. Keep your skills sharp and equipped for our rapidly changing modern world, and pay close attention to trends in your own field of work.

Investing Your Time Wisely

It may come as a surprise, especially in the context of a book geared to investments and financial planning, but your money is not the most important, or the rarest, thing you own. There is something far more important, and far more irreplaceable, than money, and that is time.

Time is the only thing you cannot buy more of. Whether you are a successful investor like Warren Buffett, a world-class entrepreneur like Mark Zuckerberg, or a starving artist still waiting for that big break, you have only so many days, months, and years on this earth. Making the most of them means setting your priorities, focusing on the things that are most important in your life, and using your time as wisely as possible.

As an avid golfer and tennis player, I invest time pursuing those passions. The exercise keeps me healthy, both physically and mentally. I have made many great friendships through my passion for sports, as I'm sure you have through your interests. As you use this book to guide your personal financial planning, do not lose sight of the fact that your money should be working for you to support how you want to be spending your time.

Do you want to spend four hours of each day in your garden and enjoy time with your children and grandchildren on the weekends? Prefer to be on a boat fishing? Want to start a new career that you're passionate about rather than retiring or continuing to work at the job that's wearing you down? Now is the time to start planning! Let's figure out how to generate enough income to support that, protect that income so that you don't ever have to give it up, and avoid the mistakes that may derail your wonderful lifestyle. If we can do that, you are truly wealthy!

Acknowledgments

Many thanks to the team of talented people at Reby Advisors who challenge themselves and me to become better fiduciary financial advisors every day. Assembling the knowledge and wisdom that positively impacts the families we touch is really a team effort and the backbone of this book.

I would also like to thank all the families and business owners we've been fortunate enough to advise as we would advise ourselves. In a dynamic and constantly changing economic landscape, as well as your constantly changing lives, we've been challenged for over three decades to meet or exceed your expectations. Thank you for your trust and confidence.

Index

N

narrow framing, 101, 110
necessities vs. desires, 54
needs vs. wants, 54
nonfinancial legacies, 169–170
nursing home care. See long-term care

O

Obamacare (Affordable Care Act), 150
optimism, 102, 112
outliving assets, avoiding, 117–132
    determining spending limit,
        118–125
    generating income, 125–132

P

pensions, 36–37, 74–75, 121
personal liability protection, 90–91
post-tax income, 78–79
public stocks, 56–60

Q

QUAIB (Quantitative Analysis of Investor Behavior), 77, 101
quality of life, 2–3

R

required minimum distributions
    (RMDs), from retirement
    accounts, 149, 167
retirement income analysis stress-tests,
    169–170
retirement savings. See also IRAs
    contributions to, 35–36
    in examples, 81–82, 129
    income taxes and, 148–150
    to leave financial legacy, 166–167
    plans for, 151–153

risks to, 128–132
    longevity, 128
    market volatility, 131–132
    sequence-of-returns, 129–131
return on behavior, 26, 40–41, 42, 73
risks
    behavioral, 99–115
        anchoring, 111
        disregarding plans, 108–109
        diversification, 110–111
        emotions, 101–104
        fear, 104–105, 113–114
        greed, 104–105, 113–114
        herding, 111
        inaction, 111–112
        loss aversion, 109
        market timing, 106–108
        media response, 112
        mental accounting, 110
        narrow framing, 110
        optimism, 112
    to lifestyle, minimizing, 27–48
        avoiding common mistakes,
            40–45
        by documenting goals, 30–32
        keeping documents up to date,
            46–47
        with liquid purpose funds,
            32–34
        by managing debt, 48
        by maximizing and protecting
            assets, 34–37
        by minimizing income taxes,
            45–46
        by protecting income, 37–40
    protecting income from, 77–78
        by choosing Medicare option,
            89–90
        disability, 82–88
        with health care strategy, 88–89
        long-term care, 92–96
        with personal liability protection, 90–91
        premature death, 82–86

About the Authors

AFTER GRADUATING FROM James Madison University with a BA in Finance in 1985, Robert J. Reby decided to pursue his passion for personal finance by founding Reby Advisors. After more than three decades in business, his vision and the firm's mission remain the same: to inspire people to achieve financial peace of mind.

Under Bob's leadership, the firm has grown from a local financial planning firm to a wealth management practice that has a national footprint with offices in Connecticut, New York, and Florida. He has been recognized by *Barron's* as one of America's Top Financial Advisors and the top independent financial advisor in Western Connecticut.

Bob has appeared on variety of media including CNN, CNBC, FOX-TV, *Business Week*, *Fortune*, *Investor's Business Daily*, Forbes. com, and many others. He was also an on-air financial specialist for "Good Morning, Connecticut," hosted "Money Sense," a weekly radio show offering financial education, and penned a weekly newspaper column of the same name for the *News Times*.

Bob is active in numerous professional organizations including the Financial Planning Association (FPA) and the World Presidents' Organization (YPO). He is also involved with numerous philanthropic organizations. Former Governor of the State of Connecticut M. Jodi

Rell recognized Bob for his service and significant contributions to the Danbury area and the State of Connecticut when she proclaimed October 6th to be Robert J. Reby & Company Day.

Bob's commitment to improving lives through financial education prompted him to author his first book, *Retire Without Worry*. His firm has been a community leader on this issue as well, hosting numerous complimentary events, including the annual economic symposium "THE ECONOMY and YOU."

Outside the office and the world of personal finance, Bob lives in Ridgefield, Connecticut, with his wife, Mary. Bob is also an avid golfer and tennis player. He has earned a national final ranking as high as 30th in the United States Tennis Association in the Senior Division.

Wealth Redefined: Charting the Way to Personal and Financial Freedom is his second book.

GREGG D. RUAIS is a managing member with Plan2Profit, a consultancy specializing in marketing and communications strategy. He has been writing professionally since 2004, collaborating with financial companies, market research firms, and numerous digital publications. He and his wife and two children live in Stamford, Connecticut.